YOU WERE CHOSEN
ON PURPOSE

From Homeless, Loss and Unsure of Your Purpose to
Healed, Whole, and Walking in Triumph

Jewel Nalls

Published by: Just Unique Love LLC

Copyright © 2025 Jewel Nalls

All rights reserved

This book is a work of nonfiction. Some names and identifying details have been changed to protect the privacy of individuals. Any resemblance to actual persons, living or dead, or actual events is purely coincidental unless otherwise indicated.

Scripture quotations are taken from the Holy Bible, New Living Translation (NLT), unless otherwise noted. Used by permission of Tyndale House Publishers.

ISBN-13: 979-8-9996365-3-9

Cover design by: Jewel Nalls

Printed in the United States of America

For more information, visit:

www.justuniquelove.com

Contact: justuniquelove@yahoo.com

To the ones who feel forgotten,

To the single mothers who press on in silence,

To the young women searching for purpose,

To the men learning how to lead with love,

To the child in you who was never taught how to survive

but did anyway...

This is for you.

And above all, to my Heavenly Father, the One who never let go of my hand, even when I couldn't see the way.

You turned every broken piece into purpose.

With love,

Jewel Nalls

TABLE OF CONTENTS

INTRODUCTION 1

CHAPTER ONE..2

CHAPTER TWO..7

CHAPTER THREE 15

CHAPTER FOUR 22

CHAPTER FIVE.. 26

CHAPTER SIX 32

CHAPTER SEVEN... 38

CHAPTER EIGHT 45

CHAPTER NINE 54

CHAPTER TEN 61

CHAPTER ELEVEN.. 69

CHAPTER TWELVE 75

CHAPTER THIRTEEN 80

CHAPTER FOURTEEN 84

CHAPTER FIFTEEN... 91

7-DAY DEVOTIONAL: CHOSEN ON PURPOSE 94

YOUR TESTIMONIES & TRIUMPHS 97

ABOUT THE AUTHOR.. 98

INTRODUCTION

"You Were Chosen on Purpose" is a powerful nonfiction memoir by Jewel Nalls that walks readers through her inspiring journey from homelessness, heartbreak, and single motherhood to healing, homeownership, and walking boldly in her God-given purpose. Through raw testimony, faith-filled moments, and transformational life lessons, Jewel proves that no matter how broken your past may be, God can rebuild your future. This book is for anyone who's ever questioned their worth, struggled to find direction, or needed a reminder that they are not forgotten they are chosen.

CHAPTER ONE

Blindfolded but Chosen
A God-Led Journey Begins

My name is Jewel, and before I share anything else, I want to thank you for picking up this book. I don't know what brought you here, but I believe it wasn't by accident. This isn't just a collection of stories it's my testimony. A journey through moments where I felt lost, unseen, and unsure of how to move forward. I didn't grow up with all the tools I needed, but I learned through the trials, and I'm still learning. Through it all, one thing has remained true: even when I couldn't feel Him, God was there. And now, I pray that what He's walked me through will somehow speak to you right where you are.

This book isn't just a story. It's a testimony. It's a journey through survival, faith, mistakes, heartbreak, healing, and the kind of growth that only God can produce. It's for the mother who feels like giving up, the young girl looking for love in the wrong places, the man who desires to lead but never had someone show him how. The person who's living life blindfolded just like I was.

I started this journey as a teenage girl who thought she had it all figured out. I wasn't taught how to handle life, love, or loss. I had to learn as I went how to drive, how to survive, how to be a mother, how to pray for real, and how to stop letting people break me just because I didn't yet know my worth.

The things I share in this book are real. They come from my handwritten journals, my prayers, my nights crying in silence, and my mornings forcing myself to keep going. But this is not the full story not yet. This book is just the beginning. The foundation.

There will be more books to come.

Each will walk you through a chapter of my life:

- One will share how I survived domestic violence
- Another how I navigated homelessness as a mother
- Another how I placed my daughter in care during a difficult time, and how that season shaped me.
- And another on how God turned my broken pieces into purpose

But for now, this is where we begin:

A girl who was 17, looking for love, searching for direction, walking through life blindfolded not knowing that every scar would one day speak to someone else's healing.

"God knew He could trust me with the scars so that in the future, I could help someone else because I've gone through it and got through it."

This is not just a book.

This is a God-led journey through truth, faith, and the kind of healing that only heaven can give.

I didn't know it then, but God had His hand on me even when I didn't feel Him. Even when I was in the wrong places with the wrong people He was still there, gently protecting me, even when I wasn't protecting myself.

At 17, I thought love was attention. I thought being wanted meant I was worthy. I didn't understand yet that real love was never supposed to hurt, confuse, or leave me feeling empty. I was looking for something someone to validate me, to anchor me, to see me when I hadn't even seen myself yet.

I didn't have a roadmap for adulthood. No one pulled me aside and said, "Jewel, slow down. You don't have to grow up this fast."

Life pushed me forward before I was ready. I was learning in real-time what it meant to survive, to adapt, and to smile through pressure.

I can still remember certain nights so vividly. Nights when I lay on someone else's couch, staring at the ceiling, asking God why I felt so misplaced. Why did I keep giving so much and getting so little in return? Why did I feel like the one no one came to check on, but everyone came to lean on?

Truth is, I was walking through life spiritually blindfolded. I didn't yet know how to recognize God's voice, and I didn't know how to trust it.

So, I leaned on feelings. On friends. On men. On temporary relief. But all those things eventually faded, and I was left with me.

A young girl with dreams but no direction.

A heart full of love but no idea how to guard it.

A spirit that was chosen but didn't yet know it.

There were signs, though. Moments that now I know were whispers from God. A last-minute job offers when I was down to my last dollar. A friend canceling plans that would've taken me to the wrong place at the wrong time. A sudden urge to journal when I felt too broken to pray.

Even when I didn't know how to ask God for help, His mercy covered me. Looking back, I realize the blindfold wasn't punishment it was protection. God was keeping me from seeing things that would've discouraged me too soon. I wasn't ready for the full picture, but He was preparing me to carry it.

I was also stubborn.

Not rebellious in a loud way but in a "I got this" kind of way.

I didn't want to seem weak. I didn't want to ask for help. I thought strength meant handling everything alone. But strength without surrender only leads to burnout.

It would take years before I truly understood that the strength I needed wasn't in me it was in God. And even more than that, it was already in me because He was in me.

The devil tried to make me feel overlooked like everyone else had a head start in life and I was already behind. But what I didn't know was that

God had delayed me to develop me. He was pruning, shaping, and preparing me to carry something weighty something holy. A testimony that would eventually help set others free.

I now understand why I had to start blindfolded because had I seen all that was ahead, I may have quit before the beauty unfolded.

But God

He allowed me to walk by faith before I even knew what faith was. And every scar, every wrong turn, every betrayal, every tear was part of a greater orchestration. One only Heaven could write.

"We do this by keeping our eyes on Jesus, the champion who initiates and perfects our faith..."

— **Hebrews 12:2 (NLT)**

✳✳✳

Some people are born into peace. Others are forged through pain. I was the latter. But I no longer see that as a disadvantage. I now know that I was chosen on purpose. Even blindfolded, I was led by a faithful God who saw the end from the beginning.

This chapter this life is not just about me. It's about the ones I'm called to reach. The women who feel unseen. The daughters walking through heartbreak. The men silently carrying burdens. The ones who need to know that even when you can't see what God is doing, He is still working.

And maybe that's you.

Maybe you're walking with a blindfold right now, wondering why life feels so heavy, so unpredictable. Can I encourage you? You're not alone.

And you're not forgotten. God specializes in walking people through seasons that feel unclear not to break them, but to build them.

He's not just trying to fix your situation — He's trying to prepare you for your assignment.

***

Reflection Prayer:

God, I may not understand everything I've been through, but I trust you.

Even when I can't see it, help me believe that You've gone before me.

Use every scar for Your glory.

Lead me even in the dark.

Amen.

CHAPTER TWO

I left with nothing but faith and my baby

There are moments in life where you don't get to plan your next move you just move. Leaving that relationship wasn't scheduled. It wasn't clean. It wasn't easy. It was survival.

I didn't leave with a plan.

I didn't leave with a support system.

I didn't even leave with clothes packed neatly in a bag.

I left with my baby in my arms and just enough faith to take the first step.

But even that wasn't simple.

The night I left, I saw my life flash before my eyes.

He had snapped. Not just in anger in violence. He came at me with a knife, screaming, trying to cut my hair off. And he did. Right there, in that moment, I didn't just feel fear I felt death breathing down my neck.

It was the final straw. I knew if I didn't get out, I might not survive. Not this time.

His sister saw what was happening and called the police. I looked him in the eyes while he stood there, knife in hand, and I said, "It's not worth it. Please, let me go."

That moment me, begging for my life became my turning point.

The police came. I was able to leave with my child, with my fear, with my shredded hair, and with the tiniest seed of faith.

And that was enough.

I called my best friend and her mother, crying, shaking, broken. And thank God, they answered. They gave me a place to stay. They didn't ask questions. They just opened the door. I stayed with them for months, trying to breathe again, trying to find out who I was after all the pain.

Eventually, I met someone new. I wasn't healed. I wasn't whole. I was still bleeding inside. But I moved in with him and his mother, trying to rebuild. His mother treated my baby girl like her own. Every morning, she would make oatmeal and feed her. That simple act felt like grace. It was the first time in a long time I had help real help with no strings attached.

They let me live there for over eight months. It wasn't perfect. But it was peaceful. I was safe. And that was a start.

The relationship with the man didn't last, but his family gave me time to reset. During that time, God opened a door I never expected: I landed a job. Not just any job a job that paid well. A job that gave me a chance to build something. That job was a miracle.

I saved. I prayed. I kept going.

And when I turned 18, I signed the lease to my very first apartment.

I held the keys in my hand and cried. It wasn't just a place to live. It was proof that I made it out. That I didn't die that night. That I was never alone, even in the worst of it. That God had His hand on me the whole time.

Even when I didn't know how to mother myself, He showed me how to mother my child.

Even when I didn't have a plan, He had one for me.

Even in chaos, He gave me glimpses of joy. Like that moment when my baby was only 3 weeks old, and we were riding in the car with her father. I looked at her, stuck my tongue out, and watched her stick hers right back out at me. At 3 weeks old. I remember thinking, "She's brilliant. She's alert. She's here with me."

She was my reminder: Keep going.

"You don't have to have it all figured out to move forward. Sometimes, faith is the only luggage you carry."

That season didn't come with ease, but it came with evidence. Evidence that God was walking with me, every step of the way.

I didn't have a rulebook for this season of my life. I was learning everything in real time. Healing and surviving at the same time are hard when you've never really seen what stability looks like. I was still hurting, still confused, still figuring out who I was. But I was determined to keep going.

I remember waking up in that house, hearing my baby's soft cry in the early morning. Some mornings I didn't want to get up. The weight of life felt heavy. But every time I saw her face, I remembered why I couldn't quit. She was innocent. She didn't ask to be here. And I was her mother.

That gave me a reason to move.

There were days I had nothing, but a small prayer whispered in my head:

"God, just give me strength today. Just today." And He did. I never went without completely. There were moments where things got tight, but I always had what I needed. Even if it was just enough. It was still enough.

Being at that house gave me breathing room. After everything I had gone through, I needed that time. I didn't talk much. I stayed to myself. I wasn't ready to open fully to anyone. I was still piecing myself back together.

I would watch his mother feed my baby, hold her, talk to her sweetly.

And I'd just sit there quiet, thanking God for placing kind people in my life, even if the relationship didn't work. She didn't treat my daughter like a burden. She didn't complain or make me feel like I overstayed my welcome. That meant more to me than she'll probably ever know.

I didn't have a lot of people checking in on me. I was a young mother, trying to start over. Some people moved on with their lives. Some didn't understand my decisions. But I was no longer looking for approval I was looking for peace.

And when that job opportunity came, it felt like a door cracked open just wide enough for me to slip through. I had no college degree. No formal experience. Just determination and a willingness to work. I showed up, and God met me there. That job changed everything.

It gave me income, but more than that, it gave me confidence. It reminded me I was capable. I could provide for my child. I didn't have to depend on anyone. I started seeing the light again even if it was just flickers at first.

I saved every check I could. I didn't have much, but I was careful with what I had. I kept reminding myself, "This is temporary. You won't always be here." And then the day came when I signed my first lease.

Eighteen years old. Holding keys in my hand. Looking at the door of my very first apartment. That moment was surreal. I remember standing in the middle of the empty room and just crying. Not because I was sad but because I was grateful. I had made it out of a nightmare. I had survived.

I wasn't just a statistic. I was a mother. I was a fighter. I was a woman choosing a different path, even if I had to take the steps trembling.

I moved in with barely any furniture. No fancy décor. But I had my daughter, and I had peace. We made that apartment our home. I made it a space of safety not just for her, but for myself too. Every day I walked through that door, I reminded myself where I had come from. And every night I locked it behind me, I thanked God I wasn't going back.

When my daughter was only three weeks old, and she mirrored my facial expression for the first time sticking her tongue out just like I did it gave me a moment of joy I'll never forget. I laughed through tears. She was growing, thriving, learning despite everything we had been through. That let me know: God was still writing our story.

I didn't have it all figured out, but I had a new beginning. And sometimes, that's more than enough.

I may have left with nothing but faith and my baby, but what I walked into was strength, resilience, and a quiet kind of victory that only God could have orchestrated.

Some nights I would lay in that apartment and just listen to the silence.

No yelling. No chaos. No fear of what mood I'd have to walk on eggshells around. That silence used to scare me at first. I wasn't used to things being still. I had become so used to surviving that peace felt foreign. But I knew deep down, this was the life I had prayed for even if it didn't look perfect on the outside.

I had my baby girl, and I had my own space. And that was more than enough.

I remember looking around at what little we had a bed, a crib, a few clothes, and not much else. But I never let that discourage me. I was just grateful to have four walls that were mine. I cleaned every corner with pride, even if there wasn't much furniture. I danced with my baby in my arms. I laughed again. Slowly, joy started returning. It didn't come all at once, but it came in pieces in small, holy moments where I could feel God saying, "Look how far you've come."

I was learning how to live, not just survive. Learning how to budget, how to cook, how to handle bills and rent and responsibilities all on my own. And it wasn't easy. But I wasn't the same girl who had to beg to be let go. I had grown. And every challenge that came with this new chapter was just another opportunity for God to show up again.

I learned how to stretch what I had. I learned how to meal prep with whatever was in my kitchen. I learned how to get creative and how to stand tall in rooms where I once would've shrunk. I was building something not just a home, but a legacy. My daughter was going to grow up watching her mother keep going, no matter what came against her.

Some days, I would just watch her sleep. Her tiny chest rising and falling.

Her peaceful little face. And I would cry quietly, not out of sadness, but out of relief. Out of gratitude. Because I almost didn't make it to see this.

That night could've gone another way. But God said, "Not so." He covered me. He made a way. And now, I had a front-row seat to watching my baby grow up in a space that wasn't full of screaming, control, or fear but filled with warmth and love.

And even though I was doing better, the healing didn't happen overnight.

There were still nights I had flashbacks. Still moments where I jumped at sudden noises or second-guessed if I was good enough. Trauma doesn't just vanish when you leave. It follows you until you make the decision to face it. And I was facing it one prayer at a time.

I would sit on the edge of my bed, talking to God out loud like He was sitting right next to me. "God, I don't know what I'm doing... but I trust you. Help me raise her. Help me heal. Help me not go back to what almost destroyed me." And He did. He met me there not when I had it all together, but when I was still in the process. And every time I opened my mouth to cry out, He answered with peace.

There were no fancy miracles. No sudden riches. Just a steady, quiet kind of favor. The kind that shows up in daily grace. In the job that kept paying. In the neighbors who smiled. In the sleep that started to come easier. In the strength to mother without giving up.

That apartment was more than a roof it was a place of restoration. It was where I started becoming me again. Where I learned how to stand on my own feet. Where I learned how to trust God not just with my emergency, but with my everyday life.

And even when things felt uncertain, I held on to that mustard seed of faith I left with. Because it had already carried me farther than I ever imagined.

Looking back, I didn't realize how strong I was while I was living it. I was just doing what I had to do. I didn't have a choice. There was no backup plan. There was no one to call for extra help. It was just me, my baby, and my faith. And sometimes, that's all you need.

People saw the outside a young girl with a child trying to make ends meet. But they didn't see the prayers I whispered walking to work. They didn't see the way I stayed up late calculating every dollar. They didn't see how hard it was to carry trauma and still show up with a smile. They didn't see how many nights I cried silently after putting my daughter to sleep, afraid of what tomorrow might bring, but still determined to get there.

But God saw.

And that's what mattered.

He saw the girl who walked away from what broke her. He saw the mother who kept showing up with love even when she was empty. He saw the daughter who was still learning how to trust Him again, even when she didn't understand why she had to go through so much. He saw me. And He kept providing. Kept covering. Kept lifting me little by little.

I didn't know then that I was planting seeds for the future version of myself. I didn't realize how the decisions I was making in that small apartment would one day become the foundation for the woman I was becoming. Every moment mattered. Every tear. Every dollar saved.

Every "yes" to responsibility. Every "no" to going back. It all mattered.

And even though that season came with hardship, it also came with glimpses of joy the kind you can't fake. The kind you only find when you've been through the fire and come out breathing.

It wasn't just that I left with nothing but faith and my baby it was that I learned faith was more than enough.

That faith led me to safety.

That faith opened doors.

That faith carried me from crisis to covering.

And years later, when I think about where I started and how far I've come, I don't see shame. I see strength. I see survival. I see the beginning of a story that God wasn't finished writing.

Because leaving didn't break me it birthed me.

CHAPTER THREE

I Had a Key, But Not a Manual

When I got my first apartment, I thought I had arrived. I had the key in my hand, a roof over my head, and a baby girl depending on me. What I didn't realize was no one gives you a manual on how to survive life when you've been surviving just to get here.

I felt proud, yes. But I also felt the pressure.

I was still in a relationship at the time, but as I started moving forward, I noticed he wasn't. He smoked all day. Laid around. No goals.

No hunger for more. And I had just come out of too much to sit still and settle. I was finally making moves, and he was fine staying stuck. So, I ended it.

But healing doesn't happen just because you're in your own place.

Sooner than later, I found myself in another relationship. I wasn't ready. But I was human. I wanted companionship, help, connection.

One night I invited my new boyfriend over, and what happened next still shakes me.

We walked into my apartment, and he stopped at the door.

"Somebody's in here," he said.

I told him he was tripping. But when I looked sure as day, my ex was lying in my bed.

I never gave him a key.

Which meant he made a spare without telling me.

I was violated. Not just physically emotionally, mentally, spiritually.

That night reminded me just how far people will go when they can't accept that you've moved on. It gave me a new kind of fear. I realized how dangerous it is when someone feels like they own you, even after you've said no.

Still, I moved on. And with my new boyfriend came stability for a while.

My daughter loved him. He treated her like she was his. He helped raise her. And we stayed together for about two years. For a moment, life felt like it was coming together.

But then Thanksgiving came and so did pain.

I was pregnant with his child. And I had a miscarriage. I didn't know it then, but God was protecting me.

Because just months later, he would be gone.

He had a sickness polyp that grew on his vocal cords. He'd been getting surgery for it since he was six years old. But by the time he needed it again, we weren't together. After the miscarriage, we had separated, still carrying grief in different ways.

He called me from the hospital.

Said he needed the surgery.

Said he was tired and just wanted to get it over with.

But I told him, "This isn't the right time. You just came off using."

He didn't care. He felt alone. And truth is, he was. His father was never in his life. His mother died of AIDS in his arms. He had no family. Just me and our past.

That night, I had a dream.

In the dream, I died but as I faded away, my body turned into his. I woke up with a knot in my chest. God had shown me.

I went back to the hospital and told him about the dream. He looked at me and said, "I had one too. I was recording myself on my phone, just in case I didn't make it... telling my people I loved them." He still insisted on the surgery. I begged him not to.

I went to work.

And that same day, the hospital called me.

He didn't make it.

They told me I was the last person he spoke to.

I rushed to the hospital. And for the first time in my life, I saw a dead body his body. Cold. Still. Gone. And all I could do was cry.

We always said we wanted to make it financially, emotionally, spiritually. We dreamed of doing better. Of surviving this world. But he didn't get to.

After he passed, my life shifted hard.

I got desperate. I had a child to take care of and bills to pay. I didn't know what to do, so I decided: I started dancing. Only for a year. Just to survive. Just to get money fast. I knew it wasn't who I was, and I knew it wasn't what God wanted for me. But I was in survival mode again not faith mode. I was numb. Hurt. Grieving. Providing.

Then one night God pulled me out.

I went in to dance like I normally did. I wasn't high. I wasn't drunk. I've never touched drugs in my life, and I didn't drink when I worked.

But while I was waiting to be called to dance, I suddenly fainted. No warning. No symptoms. Just down.

I knew instantly this wasn't physical. This was spiritual.

God was warning me: "This is not where I want to use you. You've wandered enough. It's time to clean up your mind, your self-worth, your life."

Even the house moms noticed. One looked at me one night and said, "You're different. You won't be here much longer. God has something better for you."

That was my confirmation.

And I never went back.

That was the last day I danced and the first day I started walking toward God's real purpose for my life.

"I had a key, but not a manual. But I also had God and He was teaching me, even when I didn't realize it."

This chapter of my life was full of confusion, heartbreak, and survival. But it also unlocked my calling. It revealed to me that I'm spiritually covered, even when I'm emotionally a mess. That God's voice will always reach me, even when I don't feel worthy of hearing it.

And that some of the hardest losses come right before your greatest revelations.

There was a part of my journey I haven't fully shared yet one that may shock some but will encourage many. Because even in the darkest places, I still carried the light. Even when I walked into environments I didn't belong in, I brought God with me.

When I made the decision to dance, it was never out of desire it was desperation. I was a mother with bills due, no help, and no clear direction. I had mouths to feed and rent deadlines staring me in the face. And though I knew the club wasn't where I belonged, I also knew I had to do something. Fast.

But what's powerful is this: even while I was in the club, dressed up to survive, I still shared the Word of God. I talked to other women about His goodness, even while we were in the middle of chaos. I told them there was a better way. I knew I wasn't supposed to be there, and they knew it too. I didn't drink. I didn't do drugs. I would dance, make my money, and go straight home. No hanging out. No extra conversations.

No staying late. I was terrified. Every time I entered that building, I would think, "God, please just let me make it back home to my babies."

And somehow, night after night, He did.

But eventually, that life started to eat away at my spirit. I couldn't ignore the feeling anymore. I had to make a choice. And one day, I just stopped.

No backup plan. No job waiting. Just faith. I said, "God, I'm going to trust you now. Fully. Not halfway. Not just with words. I'm going to lean on You to be my provider."

That was one of the boldest decisions I ever made.

Weeks passed. My rent was coming up, and I had no money. I had stopped dancing, hadn't found new work, and I was staring at bills I couldn't pay. I remember getting on my knees and crying out to God:

"Lord, I left what You told me to leave. I walked away in obedience. Now please come through. I need You to do what You said you would. I need You to show my children that when we trust you, you never let us down."

Days went by. Still nothing.

Then one afternoon, I went to check the mailbox not expecting anything, just routine. But there it was: a check. A large one. From a company I didn't even know still owed me money. It was enough to cover my rent that month.

I stood there frozen. Tears welled in my eyes. I knew it was God. Only He could have orchestrated that. It didn't stop there. The next month, I visited a church I'd never been to before. They were hosting a service and helping struggling families. Without asking for it, they offered to help pay my rent for the next month.

Month after month, miracle after miracle. Random deposits would appear in my account. I'd call the bank, confused, and they would tell me another company had sent funds. It didn't make sense to the world, but it made perfect sense to me. God was showing me that He was indeed my Provider and when I lean on Him, He'll move mountains for me.

That season changed me.

I began to depend more on prayer than panic. More on worship than worry. I started looking toward heaven, not people, for help. And the more I did that, the more I saw God's hand in every detail of my life.

But as I was learning to walk by faith, the enemy was still busy.

That's when I met the father of my daughter, Faith.

I was vulnerable emotionally, mentally, and spiritually and the devil always shows up when we're tired and still healing. At first, it didn't seem like a threat. It felt like companionship. He made me laugh. We had conversations. And honestly, I wanted to feel something good again. I thought maybe this time would be different.

But I didn't realize it, yet I was about to walk into another hard lesson.

One I'll talk more about later. Because even though I was growing in my faith, I was still learning that trusting God meant not just with my bills... but with my relationships too.

And that's when God began another chapter in my life one that would test everything I had just learned about trust, obedience, and purpose.

Looking back now, I understand why God allowed me to walk through that season. Not because I was being punished, but because He was preparing me. I didn't have a manual, but I had moments that became markers reminders that YAHWEH was writing my story even when I couldn't see the next page. From break-ins to heartbreaks, from pole lights to porch lights, every part of my journey was refining me. I was never meant to stay in survival mode I was meant to grow, to surrender, and to become the woman who could teach others how to trust God when they, too, feel like they're figuring it all out with just a key in their hand.

I didn't know then, but I know now I was never alone. I was being led.

CHAPTER FOUR

From the Club to Faith

After I left dancing behind, you would think life got clearer. But truth is sometimes you stop one thing and just start looking for the next thing to fill the void.

That's what I did.

I started going out more clubbing, hanging with friends, trying to keep the pain from catching up to me. I wasn't on the pole anymore, but I was still chasing validation, still running from the deep wounds inside of me. I didn't feel whole. I didn't feel loved. I felt like I needed someone. So, I went looking for "him" in all the wrong places.

That's when I met my second child's father. We met while out partying. One thing led to another, and I got pregnant. And just like the first time, I found myself doing it alone. Then it happened again.

I met another man this time also at the club and I had my third child from him. I wasn't trying to build a family like this. I was just trying to find love. But I ended up being used, betrayed, and left with more pieces to pick up. They left me with babies, and I had no choice but to become everything they weren't.

I promised God that even if the fathers left, I wouldn't leave. I would raise them, even if it broke me in the process.

With my third child's father, it seemed promising at first. I moved in with him. We were together every other night partying, living fast. I still had

God in my heart, but I was living with one foot in the world and one foot near the altar. I wasn't ready to surrender but I knew I was being pulled in two different directions.

Then came the night that changed everything.

We were supposed to go to the club, like usual. But something in me shifted. Out of nowhere, I just knew don't go tonight.

Now I understand it was the Holy Spirit.

God's voice.

A divine interruption.

So I called him and said, "I'm not going tonight. I'll wait at the house." He flipped.

Called me names. Spit on me. Cursed me out. All because I didn't want to go out like we usually did. He couldn't understand why I suddenly changed my mind. But I now know it was God protecting me.

Hours passed. He never came home.

Then the phone rang.

The hospital called.

"Do you know this person? He's been in a terrible accident. Ejected from the car. We're not sure he'll make it." My heart sank.

I rushed to the hospital. He was in ICU. Unrecognizable. And the doctors didn't think he would make it. But that wasn't the worst part.

His family the ones who never liked me shut me out completely. They told me I couldn't visit. They threw all my things out of his apartment and told me to never come back.

I was homeless again. Alone again.

But this time I was pregnant again.

When he finally got out of ICU, I called to tell him I was carrying his child.

He didn't believe me.

Hung up. Disappeared. That was it.

I was left to pick up the pieces... again.

This time, I didn't want to do it. I didn't want to keep the baby. I was overwhelmed. I felt like life kept punching me in the stomach, and I didn't have any breath left to keep standing.

So I did the only thing I could think to do I went back to my best friend and her mother.

I told her, "I don't want to keep this child."

She looked at me, didn't judge me, didn't criticize me she just prayed.

Every single day. She loved on me and lifted me back to life.

And then I heard from God.

He said, "If you keep this child, I will take care of you and your children."

And I believed Him.

I said yes.

I kept the baby.

I gave birth to a beautiful daughter. And I named her Faith because that's what it took to keep her.

It took faith to say yes when my world was falling apart.

It took faith to believe that God could turn this pain into purpose.

It took faith to know that even though I didn't have a plan, He did.

That night I didn't go to the club, God saved two lives mine and Faith's.

Had I gone, I might not be here. She might not be here.

That's how close the enemy came to stealing my destiny.

After Faith was born, I moved back into my apartment.

This time was different.

I wasn't running. I wasn't chasing.

I started walking toward God slow but steady.

I wanted to know Him deeper. To rebuild my mind. To love myself. To raise my kids with real values. I didn't have all the answers, but I had something I never truly had before:

Faith.

"When the world turned its back, God called me forward. He didn't need me to be perfect just willing. And when I said yes, He said: Now watch Me provide."

CHAPTER FIVE

Sheltered by God

After I had my daughter Faith and moved back into my apartment, I was just trying to find my rhythm again. Life felt like it was moving forward, but I was carrying the weight of so much. I had three children now. No partner. No family support. Just me, God, and whatever strength He gave me to make it through.

I was working at a call center. It wasn't my dream job, but it was enough to provide for my babies. I pushed through day after day, making sure they had what they needed. But even with all that effort, I still found myself falling behind financially.

I faced multiple evictions. Each one felt like a blow not just to my living situation, but to my credit and my confidence. My credit score dropped so low I could barely qualify for anything. And just when I thought things might level out, another storm hit literally.

There was a season of heavy rain in the area I lived. One day I went into my children's closet and saw black mold growing. Not just a little it was spreading. My babies had asthma. That kind of mold could've triggered serious health issues.

I did what any mother would do I went to the rental office to request a transfer to another unit. Their answer: "No."

They didn't care that I had no savings. No family. No backup plan. It was just "no."

A Mother at Her End

I couldn't go back to my best friend's mom's house I had already lived there twice. I wasn't speaking to any of my family, so there was no one to call for help. My only option was God.

So, I made the hardest decision I'd ever made. I packed everything I could into my small car, rented a storage unit, and started loading up.

I'll never forget carrying my baby Faith in one arm and a box in the other trying to make this impossible move work. But while going down the stairs, I slipped. I fell. I went tumbling down, holding my baby in my arms.

By the grace of God, she was okay. I was bruised physically, mentally, emotionally but somehow… still standing.

That fall wasn't just physical. It represented how low I felt. I had hit rock bottom.

But even then, God was still God.

> *"I look up to the mountains does my help come from there. My help comes from the Lord, who made heaven and earth!"*
>
> **Psalm 121:1-2 (NLT)**

Life in the Shelter

I arrived at the shelter unsure, nervous, embarrassed but desperate.

And to my surprise, they didn't turn us away. They opened the doors and gave me and my three children a room.

At first, I felt completely out of place. I had lived on my own for years. And now I was starting over, trying to learn how to crawl all over again in life.

There was no cable TV, no going out. No men were allowed. There were strict curfews and rules. But in those limitations, I found freedom to reconnect with what truly mattered: God and my children.

I started reading my Bible at night. I attended church on Sundays. I began to shut out the distractions of the world and lock in on God.

And something started to shift.

My Children, My Mirror

That's also when I started to pay closer attention to my children to who they were in this season of struggle.

My firstborn daughter was an angry child. Even as a baby, she cried a lot. She was smart extremely smart but always troubled. She had been my only child for three years before I had my son. And it was like she couldn't accept sharing my love and attention.

When it was just me and her, she clung to me. If I tried to rest or have a moment to myself, she'd bang on the door, yell, act out just to make sure she had my attention. And to be honest, I wasn't with her 24/7.

I used to club a lot. But when I wasn't out, I was with her, loving her, feeding her, caring for her. Still, she was always upset.

Any daycare or school I sent her to she got kicked out the first week. She bullied other children. No one wanted to watch her. And after I had my son, it got worse.

My son, on the other hand, was quiet. Gentle. Sweet. He rarely cried.

So was Faith. Smart and calm peaceful babies. But my firstborn? She was my daily reminder that pain doesn't skip children.

I was only 18 trying to raise a child who didn't know how to process what she was feeling, and I didn't know how to help her. But I see now she was just responding to all the chaos she'd witnessed, felt, and absorbed. She wanted me. She needed me whole. And I was still becoming.

As I spent more time in the shelter, I began to realize this wasn't punishment. It was preparation.

God was using this space to cleanse me. To press me. To mold me into someone stronger, wiser, more patient. He was building my character and rebuilding my heart.

> *"We can rejoice, too, when we run into problems and trials, for we know that they help us develop endurance. And endurance develops strength of character, and character strengthens our confident hope of salvation."*
>
> **— Romans 5:3–4 (NLT)**

I couldn't club anymore. I couldn't party or date or distract myself. I had no choice but to sit in the silence and listen to God.

And in that stillness, He started revealing things to me.

That I was chosen.

That I was set apart.

That I wasn't supposed to fit in because I was created to stand out.

To lead. To heal. To break chains. To help others.

During my year of stay in that shelter, one of the requirements was to attend financial literacy classes. At first, I thought it was just another thing to check off the list—just another rule to follow in this new chapter I didn't ask to be in. But the more I sat through those classes, the more I realized how necessary they were. They weren't just teaching us how to budget they were showing us how we ended up here in the first place.

I had never really been taught how to manage money. I just knew how to survive. I knew how to pay what was due that day and figure out the rest later. But surviving and stewarding are two different things. These classes broke down everything credit, saving, planning, needs versus wants. They made me confront my spending habits, my mindset, and the roots of some of my financial decisions. I had to look in the mirror and accept accountability, not shame.

The teacher, a woman who had once been homeless herself, said something that stuck with me: "This isn't about blame. It's about change." And for the first time, I started to believe that maybe I could build something stable not just for me, but for my children.

I remember sitting in those classes, baby Faith in my lap, taking notes with a broken pen and a borrowed notebook, thinking: "One day, I'm going to teach this to somebody else. One day, I'm going to tell my story not from a place of pain, but from a place of purpose."

God was using that shelter to build more than just a roof over my head He was building a new foundation under my feet.

And through that year, I didn't just learn about finances. I learned about faith, discipline, and identity. I learned how to dream again. I learned that being broke doesn't mean you're broken. And that sometimes, the best things in life begin at your lowest point.

This shelter wasn't just a temporary stop. It became the soil where God started planting seeds in me seeds that would soon bloom into something I never imagined.

"You didn't choose me. I chose you. I appointed you to go and produce lasting fruit..."

— John 15:16 (NLT)

———

Covered in the Valley

I thought the shelter was the end. But it was the place where I found the beginning of my calling.

God had me covered. Even when it felt like I had nothing, He was everything.

"The Lord is a shelter for the oppressed, a refuge in times of trouble."

— Psalm 9:9 (NLT)

This chapter of my life reminded me: sometimes, God must strip you of the world... so you can finally become who He created you to be.

CHAPTER SIX

God of the Details

Living in a homeless shelter wasn't something I ever imagined for myself. But there I was—three children in tow, no family to call on, and nothing but faith to carry me through. The shelter gave us a roof, yes, but it was far from easy.

They allowed us to stay for 12 months a full year to get back on our feet. The first stage was humbling. We lived in a cold, office-like building, sharing space with other women and children in crisis. No TVs. No privacy. The beds were hard as bricks. It felt more like a holding cell than a home. My daughter Faith ended up catching a staph infection while we lived there, and that broke me. Watching her little body suffer made me question everything my decisions, my strength, even my prayers.

But I didn't stop believing. I didn't stop seeking God.

One day, the counselor called me in and said, "If you can save up $1,000, we'll move you to the next phase a transitional shelter. You'll have your own one-bedroom apartment. It's more comfortable, and we'll only take 30% of your income. The rest you must save to prepare for moving into your own permanent place." That was all I needed to hear.

I went out and got a job at IHOP. I knew I had to serve, even in my brokenness. Funny how God kept placing me in positions of serving feeding people physically when one day I knew I'd be feeding them spiritually.

In just one month, I saved $1,000. That wasn't me that was God.

Customers would tip me with favor like I'd never seen before. I wasn't just serving food; I was walking in purpose without even realizing it.

"The generous will prosper; those who refresh others will themselves be refreshed."

— Proverbs 11:25 (NLT)

When I showed the counselor my bank statement, she looked at me with disbelief. "You really did it," she said. "You're ready."

I moved into the transitional shelter my own little one-bedroom apartment. It wasn't much, but it was clean, quiet, and finally... mine. I had space to breathe. I had space to heal.

I kept working at IHOP and raising my babies. And every day, I felt like God was gently shifting my life into a new season. There were still struggles, yes. But something had shifted inside me. I no longer felt like I was just surviving I was starting to grow again.

But the clock was ticking. My 12 months in the program were almost up, and it was time to find permanent housing. And that's when fear tried to creep back in.

I had two evictions on my credit. A score so low that no apartment complex wanted to take a chance on me. I applied to multiple places. Every one of them denied me.

That's when I went back to the One who had never denied me. I went back to my prayer room the quiet space in my spirit, and I poured out everything to God.

I prayed:

"Lord, you see what I'm facing. I've done the work. I've trusted you. I've applied, I've waited, I've hoped. Now I need You to show me the next move. Don't let me be homeless again. Lead me, God. Where do You want me to live next?"

And just days later, He answered.

At 4am, I woke up from a vivid dream. In it, I saw a city I had never heard of and a beautiful brick building. The name of the city was clear. The building was clear. I had no idea where it was, but I knew God had just revealed something important.

I wrote the name down in my dream journal and went back to sleep.

That morning, I searched the city name online, using a rental website that showed apartments across different counties. And there it was.

The exact city. The exact building.

The same one from my dream.

I clicked on the listing, called the number, and was directed to fill out an application online.

Five minutes after submitting it I was approved.

They only asked for a $500 deposit.

No long screening process.

No judgment.

Just a green light from heaven.

And at that moment, I wept. Not out of sadness but because I was finally seeing what it meant when people say: God is in the details.

I had applied to so many places and been denied. But God had one specific place reserved just for me.

"When people's lives please the Lord, even their enemies are at peace with them."

— Proverbs 16:7 (NLT)

God made a way that no man could block. He gave me a home when I had no idea where I'd go. He opened a door that no one else could open.

And from that day forward, I made a vow: I will never again doubt what God can do.

He had brought me through homelessness heartbreak poverty loss and now He was restoring me.

One brick building at a time.

I had never driven so many miles with such uncertainty but also such peace. The city was new, unfamiliar, and far from everything I once called home. But something in my spirit said, "This is it. This is where I'm planting you." It wasn't just a place to rest it was a place to rebuild. I didn't know many people there, but I did have one small thread of connection my sister, who was going to college about thirty minutes away. Just knowing she was nearby gave me a bit more courage to step into the unknown.

I remember pulling up to the building with my kids in the backseat. It looked exactly like the vision God gave me. Brick by brick, detail by detail. It was like He carved it out in the spirit before it ever appeared in the natural. That's when I knew this wasn't just about getting housing. This was about destiny alignment. God didn't just lead me to shelter; He led me to the city of promise.

When I unlocked the front door and walked into our new apartment, I stood in the middle of the empty living room and cried. Not because I was sad but because I was seen. God had seen me. Every prayer. Every sleepless night. Every whispered hope. He hadn't forgotten a single one. I finally felt like I had entered the land He promised me.

The children ran through the rooms with excitement. No more curfews.

No more shared spaces. No more asking permission to live. This was our home. A fresh beginning. A safe space. A chance to start over on solid ground.

And here's what made it even more miraculous: I didn't have to compromise to get it. I didn't have to beg or twist the truth or push past rejection. I waited on God and He showed up right on time.

After we settled in, I went outside, sat on the front step, and looked up at the sky. And I whispered:

"God You really are in every detail."

Because only He could take a broken girl, shelter her through storms, teach her to save, push her into transition, and then plant her in a new land without her lifting anything but a prayer.

He really is the God who prepares the place before He moves the person.

That move was a pivot point in my life. It wasn't just a physical relocation it was a spiritual elevation. It was the beginning of God not just answering my prayers but trusting me with more. And I didn't take that lightly.

That new city became the training ground for the woman I was becoming. And even though I couldn't see the full picture yet, I knew He was painting something beautiful.

Because every season I thought would break me only built me.

And in the background of it all, God was writing the blueprint of my destiny. Line by line. Detail by detail.

CHAPTER SEVEN

The hardest decision I ever made

After I got into my new apartment in a new county and city I'd never heard of. Remind you I didn't move here because of family moved here out of faith after God showed me my next move. I was in a very unfamiliar place. But this place turned out to be the best place you could ever raise a child. And succeed in life..

All the kids were on board with it except my oldest daughter, Jaliya.

She hated it, and it showed toward me, the schools, and her siblings. She was having a very hard time adjusting. She had family in the town I was raised in on her dad's side. She loved living in the place I had left but I couldn't succeed there. The school system was horrible. There was a lot of theft and violence. I left that place for the better. I was also trying to escape my abusive children's father.

Things took a hard turn when we settled into our apartment. Jaliya started behaving badly in school. She disobeyed house rules, refused to do her chores, and became angry when I wouldn't take her places. When she got upset, she took her pain out on herself and the entire house to the point where she became suicidal.

One day, she took six pills and tried to end her life. She was so torn over the fact that her dad had never been there for her and hated living in the new place God had led me to. She also said I was overprotective and didn't let her do anything.

I raised her in my home until she was 16. I let her live with her grandmother at age 13 because her behavior had become so disruptive. I placed her in counseling and exhausted every resource the county provided. She didn't even want to attend the meetings. Some days, she would stand in front of me and curse because she was bored. She broke TVs, banged on windows, and ran away several times.

One time, she ran away and led the police on a foot chase. They eventually found her in my next-door neighbor's home I didn't even know she was there until the police located her at school the next day.

She ran away numerous times. She even choked her brother in the kitchen, and I had to get her Baker Acted. It became a monthly cycle. She cut herself several times.

One day it got very dangerous she grabbed a knife when I told her I was calling the police again for help. I didn't know what she was going to do. I felt like my life and the lives of my other four children were in danger. The police came and took her under the Baker Act.

She stayed with her grandmother for a year and a half. But one night at 3 AM, her grandmother called and begged me to come get her. She said, "I don't care what you do with her place her in foster care, but she can no longer live with me." Jaliya had broken things in her home and was acting out again.

Jaliya can be both loving and angry. I prayed over her, talked to her, tried to reach her. She would be nice for a while, then snap again. That last day, when she pulled the knife and said it wasn't for us but for the police that was it. The police arrested her, and Baker Acted her once more.

I prayed to God. I told Him I was tired. We had no help. No family.

No village. I didn't want to pick her back up again, but I felt all our lives were at risk. I didn't want my other children to think her behavior was acceptable or feel like they could do the same to me. I didn't want to sleep with one eye open every night.

Counseling didn't work. Her grandmother couldn't manage her.

Nothing worked. I felt stuck unable to move forward mentally, spiritually, or emotionally.

Leaving my child in that facility was the hardest decision I've ever had to make. But I prayed and I let go. I had to let God.

The day she grabbed that knife, I felt something shift in me.

It wasn't the first time things had gotten bad, but this time it felt different.

Darker. Heavier. She wasn't just yelling or breaking things she had a weapon in her hand. And even though she said it wasn't for us, the fact that she even had it the fact that I didn't know what she might do... that was enough. I had five children in that home. And in that moment, I knew I couldn't wait for something worse to happen.

I called the police.

I had called them before, but this time felt like a final cry for help. I stood in the kitchen holding my breath while they walked through the door, praying she wouldn't do anything reckless not to them, not to herself, and not to me.

They took her under the Baker Act again. I didn't fight it. I didn't beg. I didn't even speak much. I just nodded and let them do what they had to do. Because in that moment, I didn't feel like her mother... I felt like the only line of protection left for the rest of my kids.

I went into my room that night and just sat in silence. I stared at the wall, mind racing but body frozen. I was mentally stuck. I didn't want to bring her back home. I couldn't.

I didn't feel safe.

My kids didn't feel safe.

And I didn't feel like I had any options left.

I kept thinking, What kind of mother leaves her child in a facility? But then I thought, What kind of mother puts the rest of her children at risk just to prove she didn't give up?

I had tried. God knows I had tried.

The counseling. The programs. The space. The grace. The prayers. The begging. The boundaries. The patience. I had done everything I knew to do. I had reached the end of myself. I didn't have anything left but prayer.

So I prayed one more time.

I told God, "If You want me to bring her back, you're going to have to make that clear. Because I don't see a way forward if this continues. I don't want to pick her back up just to go through the same cycle. I'm tired. My other children are afraid. I'm doing this alone."

And as hard as it was to say I meant it.

I couldn't keep letting her come home, cause damage, get taken away, and come back like nothing happened. I wasn't helping her by doing that.

I was enabling her. I was trying to hold her together, and in the process, I was falling apart. I had to start recording things.

I installed cameras in my own home not because I wanted to invade anyone's privacy, but because I was genuinely scared. I needed proof. I needed to protect myself and my other children. I told myself, if something ever happens... if this ends up on Channel 7 News at least they'll know the truth.

She would stand inches away from my face nose to nose screaming and cursing at me like I was some girl off the street, not the mother who gave her life. The disrespect was something I had never imagined I would deal with. And all of it? Over little things. I wouldn't take her somewhere when she wanted to go, and suddenly I was the worst person in the world.

I'd ask her to do the dishes, and she'd explode. She'd wake up in a mood, and the entire house would feel it before breakfast.

I'd ask her, "What's going on with you? Why are you so angry?"

Her answer was always the same: "I'm bored. I don't have a dad. You don't let me do anything."

I'd hear it repeatedly that I was too strict, that I ruined her life, that she didn't want to be in this new city. And no matter how much I tried to help her understand why I made the decisions I made, she didn't want to hear it.

She took small things and made them major. Minor instructions turned into full-blown arguments. I couldn't ask her to clean up after herself without being accused of controlling her. I couldn't say no without getting punished emotionally for it. Her attitude would spread through the house like poison. And by the end of the day, we were all walking on edge again.

I reached out to the county so many times I lost count. I called every number I could find. I asked for counselors, mentors, programs, wraparound services anything. And I followed through. I signed forms. I showed up for every meeting. I tried it all.

But nothing worked.

Even the police officers who came to the house regularly they started recognizing her name before I even finished explaining. They would nod and say, "We know her." But they never had answers. They had no advice. They had no solutions. They were just as lost as I was.

I felt helpless. Completely worn out. How do you mother a child who fights you like an enemy?

It wasn't just that I was out of options it was that I was out of energy. Out of trust. Out of strength.

The day I left her in that facility, I didn't feel like a bad mother. I felt like a mother who had tried everything.

I wasn't giving up on her I was giving her to God.

I had to. Because if I didn't, I was going to lose myself. I was going to lose the safety and structure I had worked so hard to build for my other children. And I couldn't risk that.

It wasn't a lack of love. It was the deepest kind of love the kind that says,

I can't help you the way you need anymore... but I can still love you from afar while I protect the rest of us.

I knew she wouldn't understand it in the moment. I knew she might even hate me for it. But one day, I believe she'll look back and realize it took everything in me to make that decision.

And the truth is it was the hardest decision I've ever made.

Not because I didn't have peace about it. But because I never thought I would be in that position. No mother dreams about the day she has to leave her child in the hands of the state. But when you've exhausted every resource, every phone call, every tear, and every ounce of strength... sometimes obedience looks like letting go.

I went home that night with an emptiness in the house, but a strange calm in my spirit. For the first time in years, my other children were able to sleep in peace. There was no screaming. No chaos. No fear. It was quiet.

And I didn't feel guilty I felt covered.

Because I had prayed.

I had fasted. I had tried. I had loved hard. And God knew I had done all I could.

I still prayed for her. I still missed her. I still wanted her to be whole. But I finally understood that healing wouldn't happen in my home it had to happen in God's hands.

This wasn't rejection this was release.

And I trust that if God could lead me out of abuse, out of poverty, out of homelessness, and into peace then He could lead her too.

Maybe not through me, but through someone. Somehow.

So I closed that chapter with a heavy heart but with full faith.

Because sometimes the strongest thing a mother can do is let go and let God.

CHAPTER EIGHT

When I gave it to God

After Jaliya went into foster care, there was an unfamiliar quiet in the house. A peace settled over me and the kids something we hadn't experienced in a long time. It wasn't easy, but when you are not of this world and you give your burdens to God, something changes. Once God assists you in making a decision, you no longer stress about it after. I left it in His hands and that's where my strength came from.

My youngest daughter, only three at the time, carried the weight of the trauma with her. She went to school months later and told her teacher what she remembered: her sister pulling a knife. I realized then how deeply things had impacted all my children. But even through that, we all had peace. I still called to check on Jaliya and sent support when I could. I wanted her to know I still loved her, that I was still her mom. I just didn't have the capacity to give her the mental help she needed. That didn't mean I stopped praying for her.

During this time, God began opening major doors for me. I told my children I would get a new truck one day, and they watched me hustle and trust God until it happened. But before that came another miracle.

I was blessed with the opportunity to own a home through Habitat for Humanity. It was a divine moment one I'll never forget. One day, a new woman was hired at the restaurant I worked at. She was also a server. She randomly mentioned, "You should apply for a home through

Habitat for Humanity." I hadn't told her anything about my living situation or desires. It felt like she was sent straight from Heaven. The same week she said that she was gone. I never saw her again. I truly believe she was an angel.

I followed through, applied for the program, and a month later, I was approved. Not only was I selected, but they also chose me to be the featured family for their Women Build event. They said my story inspired them how I was raising my children, how I hadn't given up.

Women entrepreneurs from all over Florida came to help build my home. I was nine months pregnant at the time, but I still showed up to help put nails in my walls and paint my future. The build was completed in just three months right before the pandemic began.

While living in the city God led me to, I met the father of my youngest child. He planted the seed that led me to start my own property-based business. Though our relationship didn't last, I know God used him to teach me how to walk into entrepreneurship and independence.

Three years after obeying God's instruction to move, I owned a brand-new home, a business, a reliable truck, and I had peace in my heart. My credit had improved. My family was stable. My faith was strong. My life was unrecognizable from what it once was.

Even with all this, I never stopped praying for Jaliya. Because when you truly give something to God, you trust He will handle it in His time, His way.

I started realizing that giving something to God isn't just a one-time decision it's a daily one. Every time I felt that pressure rising, every time a thought of doubt tried to creep back in, I had to choose to surrender again. "Lord, you brought me this far. I trust you to carry the rest."

I didn't need to know when or how Jaliya's breakthrough would happen. I just needed to stay in position. I stayed in prayer. I stayed obedient. I stayed available for when God would open the next door for her, for me, for all of us.

There was such a deep relief in finally being able to breathe again in my own home. To wake up and not immediately feel tension. To hear my younger children playing, laughing, being kids — without the fear of an outburst or another emergency. That peace wasn't something I took for granted. It was a gift. One I had been praying for. One that cost me so much to finally walk in.

And I wasn't perfect in the process. There were days I questioned myself. Days I wondered if she'd ever understand why I made the decisions I did. Days I had to remind myself, "This doesn't mean you failed. This means you were strong enough to make a decision no one else could."

Strength doesn't always look like keeping everything together sometimes it looks like releasing what's breaking you.

And in that season of release, God honored my obedience in ways I could've never imagined. The home. The truck. The business. All of it came after I truly gave the situation over to Him. It was like God had been waiting on me to finally let go so He could show me what He had planned all along.

I started my property-based business with no blueprint, no background, and no savings. Just knowledge passed down, a little guidance from someone who came into my life for a season, and faith. Pure faith. The same faith that got me into that apartment. The same faith that got me approved for a home. The same faith that helped me raise children with nothing but love, prayer, and consistency.

Even when the relationship with my youngest child's father ended, I didn't fold. Because I had already learned not to rely on people for what only God can provide. I didn't beg anyone to stay. I didn't force connections. I knew my identity wasn't in who was with me it was in who had sent me.

God had called me to stability. And this time, I wasn't going to lose it trying to hold on to people who weren't assigned to stay.

I stayed focused. I started showing up for myself differently. I managed my time better. I got more intentional with my children. I made sure they felt secure again. And they started to respond with more trust, more peace, and more joy. I could see the difference in their eyes.

I made space for structure again morning routines, after-school talks, family meals, and more stillness. I even started to take better care of myself. I didn't want to just survive anymore. I wanted to enjoy life. I wanted to enjoy my children. I wanted to smile and mean it.

And I did.

I would walk through my new home and pause sometimes, just to soak it in. It wasn't the biggest house, but it was mine. I remembered all the times I prayed for a safe place to raise my babies and now I was walking in the promise. I remembered the times I cried wondering if I'd ever have peace again and now, I was living in it.

That's what happens when you give it to God. You stop surviving on your own strength, and you start seeing results only He can produce.

And even with all the blessings that came after, the thing I held on to the most was peace.

I could finally rest at night. Not because everything was perfect but because I had let go of what wasn't mine to carry. I had stopped replaying the past and started protecting the present.

And that's what my children needed. They didn't need me to fix everything. They needed me to be present. Focused. Whole. They needed a mother who wasn't weighed down by guilt or fear, but who could lead them with clarity and love. And that's exactly who I was becoming.

All because I gave it to God.

Even though I had given it to God, I still thought about Jaliya almost every single day. I didn't leave her behind emotionally — I carried her with me in prayer, in thought, and in every decision I made. I used to tell her when she was younger, "Just hold on I'm going to give us a better life. It's coming. God promised it." And I meant it. I wanted her to be a part of this legacy. I wanted her to witness the promise unfold not just from a distance, but by walking in it too.

When she entered foster care, we didn't speak for a month. But I never stopped checking on her after that. I stayed in contact and continued to support her in the ways I could. I was praying the time apart would give her wisdom. That maybe the separation would help her grow and reflect that she would begin to understand how to handle the things in life she couldn't control. I was hoping that eventually, we'd come back together, and she'd be able to live in the promise that God gave us.

And then came the moment I had waited for: she turned eighteen. She aged out of the system. I saw a glimmer of light in her a little more selfawareness, a little calmer. She smiled more. She seemed freer. So, I asked her if she wanted to come back home.

And she said yes.

I wanted to believe this was our second chance a new beginning. I wanted restoration. I wanted peace. So, I gave her another shot, not just for her, but for both of us.

For her 18th birthday, I helped her purchase her very first car. She contributed a small portion, and I paid the rest as I had promised her I would. I helped her launch her business. I supported her efforts to get paid through her online presence. I poured into her not just as a mother, but as a builder trying to set her up with tools so she wouldn't have to depend on this world or anyone in it. I gave her structure. I gave her support. I gave her everything I could to help her succeed.

But even with all of that, she still looked at me with anger.

I asked her several times if she had forgiven me if she truly understood why I had placed her in foster care. We talked. We both cried. We shared our perspectives. And for a while, I thought healing was finally coming between us. But over time, the atmosphere in the house shifted again. A dark cloud returned. The energy felt heavy. Familiar.

Then she started talking to someone a man.

At first, I didn't know who he was. She was secretive about it. I'd hear her on the phone with him for hours, and every time I asked, she brushed me off. I felt something in my spirit wasn't right.

One day, someone reached out anonymously and asked if I knew who my daughter was talking to. They gave me his full name and told me to search him up. I had already asked her multiple times she never gave me a straight answer. But before I even searched him, God had already shown me this man in a dream.

In that dream, I saw his age. I saw how he looked. I even heard how he talked to her. When I described all of it to Jaliya, she broke down crying.

She was shocked that God had revealed what she had tried to hide. The truth came out.

She told me he was the man she had gone on a date with while she was still in foster care when she was 17. And he was 31.

My heart dropped.

I told her straight up this isn't right. That's not love. That's manipulation.

That's illegal. I tried to speak wisdom to her, not with judgment, but with protection. I said, "He only wants one thing from you. A real man wouldn't be looking at a teenage girl." But she didn't want to hear it.

She didn't listen.

And even though I had given so much... the peace I had worked to protect began to unravel again.

After all this started to unravel again, I sat her down and told her the truth not just as her mother, but as a woman who had lived it.

I told her, "Men like this will keep moving around you. This is a cycle.

Your father met me when I was 17 and he was 27. I ran away from that pain. I lived that heartbreak. I already know how this ends." I was trying to protect her from what I had already survived. I didn't want her to go through what I had gone through.

But like before, she didn't listen.

I warned her, "Be careful. Don't let this man get too close. Don't let him know where we live. Men like that will put a GPS on your car. They'll follow you. They'll track you." And then she told me something else he was a scammer. That was it for me. I didn't want him anywhere near my home, near my kids, or near the peace I had worked so hard to rebuild. Day by day, I started to not want her in the home anymore.

Not because I didn't love her but because she was living too recklessly.

And with both of us being very visible on social media, I had to move with wisdom and protection. I had other children to protect. Our safety mattered. And the peace in my home mattered.

Her high school graduation was coming up. She told me she only had tickets for me and my second oldest child. She didn't want to bring the other three. She said she didn't want to be bothered with them. On top of that, the man the same man I had warned her about was going to be attending.

Her graduation was over four hours away. And just a week before the event, we got into another argument. Out of nowhere, she texted me:

"Don't come to my graduation." Then she blocked me. Off her phone.

Off every social media page. Gone.

And I made another painful decision.

I didn't go.

Not because I didn't love her.

Not because I wasn't proud.

But because she had made it clear she didn't want me there. Because I wasn't going to leave my younger children behind for days just to sit beside a man who was grooming her. Because she blocked me and held the tickets. Because no matter how hard it was, I had to choose peace again.

That moment broke me a little more.

But I chose, once again, to give it to God.

She got angry when someone later asked why I didn't attend. I told the truth. Calmly. Honestly. And that made her even more upset. So upset, she started exposing private, personal information. She shared things that could have put our safety at risk.

And that was my last straw.

I had forgiven. I had opened my doors. I had poured out every resource and every ounce of love I had. I had been patient. I had prayed. But I couldn't walk with her while she was choosing chaos. I couldn't make excuses anymore. I couldn't let her pain put the rest of us in danger.

So I gave it all back to God.

Again.

Not in defeat but in surrender.

Not because I stopped loving her but because I finally loved myself enough to let God finish what I couldn't fix.

―――

"Give all your worries and cares to God, for He cares about you."
— *1 Peter 5:7 (NLT)*

Letting go doesn't mean walking away forever. It means choosing peace while still praying for healing. It means trusting that even when it hurts,

God still has a plan. And this time, I'm not moving in guilt. I'm moving in grace.

Because when I gave it to God... I gained peace.

And I'm not letting that go.

CHAPTER NINE

Peace in a Place God Promised

I still remember walking into that neighborhood for the first time. It was exactly what I saw in my dream brick buildings, peace in the atmosphere, and a quiet stillness that told me: this is it. God had spoken, and here I was, standing in the manifestation of His Word.

The day I signed the closing documents felt like a full-circle moment. After all the nights I cried myself to sleep in the shelter, all the evictions, all the moments I had to encourage myself just to keep going I was now holding the keys to a home I didn't even qualify for in the natural. But God doesn't operate on credit scores; He operates on obedience and faith.

I had brought money with me that day for the closing costs. I wanted to be prepared. But when I sat down at the table, they told me everything was covered. The grant had taken care of it all. My eyes welled up with tears. I couldn't even speak. All I could do was whisper in my heart, "Thank You, Lord." God had once again done what only He could do He made a way where there was absolutely no way.

I was approved through Habitat for Humanity, which allowed me to finance the home interest-free. That meant every payment I made went straight to the principal. My mortgage, including taxes and insurance, came out to just $708 a month. For the first time in my adult life, I could breathe. I could save. I could plan. I could give.

Although landscaping and the business God had helped me start still had seasonal highs and lows, I no longer feared losing my home. My bills were affordable, and my faith was stronger than ever. I wasn't rich in money, but I was rich in peace and peace is priceless.

Soon after moving in, I gave birth to my last child. It was a fresh start in every way. A new home. A new baby. A new season of stability. A new chapter in my walk with God. I was growing emotionally, spiritually, and mentally. But even in that joy, there was a silent ache in my heart my daughter Jaliya.

I would sit on the floor in prayer, praying deeply for her healing. Our journey hadn't been easy. There were moments where the spiritual warfare felt intense so thick it could be felt in the room. One day, she looked at me with a blank expression and said, "I want to be better than Jesus."

My heart shattered. I didn't yell. I didn't panic. I knew that wasn't her speaking. That was the enemy trying to distort her mind. I gently responded, "That's not you talking, baby. That's a spirit, and we're going to pray against that." I could see how much she was struggling on the inside. And I also knew that her healing wouldn't come from me alone it would come from God. All I could do was release her back into His hands.

While trusting God for my daughter's restoration, I focused on being a good steward over everything else He had blessed me with. I became more hands-on with the landscaping and property preservation work. The father of my last child had taught me how to install sod, plant flowers, edge sidewalks, and transform yards. I didn't just watch I learned. I practiced. I applied. I used those skills to maintain my own yard. My own property. It felt good to walk outside and see the fruit of my hands.

Looking back, I realize that season wasn't just about learning how to work outside. It was about learning how to build from the inside out. God was teaching me that I didn't need to depend on anyone to create beauty around me I could do it myself with His guidance. He was showing me how to be rooted. How to cultivate what He placed in my hands.

And I can't forget the angel God sent me during my waiting season. While I was working as a server just trying to make ends meet a woman I barely knew leaned over and said, "You should apply for Habitat for Humanity." She wasn't even supposed to be there that day. In fact, after that conversation, I never saw her again. I believe she was a divine messenger. A planted vessel. A whisper from heaven to push me toward the promise.

God used everything the delays, the disappointments, the detours to direct me right where I needed to be. He reminded me that He doesn't just drop blessings out of the sky. He builds them brick by brick, in His perfect time.

That home wasn't just a house. It was a sanctuary. A covering. A testimony. A physical representation of what it means to walk by faith and not by sight. I didn't qualify by man's standards, but I was chosen by God.

That's when the idea was planted in my heart to begin sharing my testimony on a larger scale. I didn't know how, or when, or what it would look like, but I knew I had to share what God had done for me. Because if He could take a single mother, homeless and broken, and place her in a home of peace and promise He could do it for anyone.

I often say this to myself: "Never stop giving God your yes even when it's hard." Because behind every yes is a door you didn't even know was waiting to open.

This wasn't just peace in a house this was peace in the purpose God promised.

Although everything wasn't perfect, for the first time in a long time, I felt safe. I had a door that locked, a space that was mine, and children who could run freely through rooms that I had prayed for. I decorated slowly, turning this house into a home filled with laughter, scripture, and rest. My children had their own rooms. I could cook dinner without watching over my shoulder. I could sit on my porch and feel the breeze without wondering where we'd go next.

God didn't just give us shelter. He gave us peace.

But even with all that peace, I never forgot the journey. I would often walk through my home and silently thank God for the walls around me, the floor beneath me, the roof above my head. I had seen the lowest valleys, but now I was living in a promise that He had revealed to me in a dream.

I remember looking at my daughters one day, watching them do homework at the kitchen table, and I just stood there still, grateful, overwhelmed. They had stability now. We weren't couch-hopping, moving from place to place, or living out of a storage bin. We were home.

And though my oldest, Jaliya, couldn't enjoy the full six and a half years we lived here, she witnessed enough to be able to know who to call on when times get hard. She saw her mother fall to her knees in prayer. She saw provision come out of nowhere. She watched the way I spoke to God out loud, the way I held on to scripture, and the way I never gave up, even when it looked like everything around me was falling apart. Seeds were planted.

Even if she didn't say it, I know those moments left an imprint. That matters more to me than any possession in this home. I didn't want to just give my children a place to live I wanted to give them a legacy of faith.

And that's what God was doing: building legacy, one step at a time.

As time passed, I found myself growing in confidence and leadership. I was no longer that scared young mother hiding behind prayers. I was walking in them. I was building my own tables. I was trimming hedges and installing mulch in my own yard. I didn't wait for help I became the help. And the same tools I used in the natural, God was teaching me how to use spiritually.

I remember working on a lawn job one morning, the sun beaming down on my shoulders, sweat pouring from my forehead, and I whispered to God, "Thank You. Even for this." Because even in the hard work, I saw Him. I had strength to do what I once thought I couldn't. I was a mother, a businesswoman, a homeowner, a vessel and all of it was led by faith.

And slowly, the dream God showed me began to make more sense. This city. This brick building. This community. It wasn't just about a house. It was about foundation. He was establishing something through me that my children and grandchildren could build on. This was legacy in real time.

I started budgeting differently. I became more intentional about giving, tithing, and sowing into others. I knew what it felt like to need help, and I wanted to be someone who could give help now that I was able to do so. I also began to explore new dreams ones I didn't have time or mental space to entertain before. I thought about mentoring young mothers. Starting a journal club. Launching a devotional series. I even began writing my own book this one you're reading now because I knew the same God who rescued me could use my voice to help rescue others.

And it all started with peace.

Peace in a place He promised. Peace that wasn't loud or showy. Peace that looked like slow mornings, paid bills, and children laughing in the backyard. Peace that wrapped itself around me like a warm blanket, assuring me I was no longer in survival mode. I was finally walking in purpose.

Not perfection purpose.

There were still challenges. There were moments I had to war in prayer. There were times I had to rebuke doubt and fear that crept in when I looked too far ahead. But even in those moments, I remembered the day I moved in how I stood in the doorway and whispered, "Thank You, God."

He didn't just deliver me. He settled me. And in that settlement, I found rest.

This chapter of my life showed me what happens when you wait on God. When you trust His voice over the noise. When you follow Him even when the map isn't clear. He doesn't just give you a place to live. He gives you space to breathe. To rebuild. To believe again. This home wasn't just an address it was evidence that He never forgot about me.

Even in my darkest hour, He was building something beautiful.

Even when I didn't know how He did.

Even when I didn't feel worthy He still made a way.

And now, every time I look around this home, I don't just see rooms and furniture I see faith fulfilled. I see restoration. I see the beginning of generational change.

This was the house that peace built.

And this was only the beginning.

CHAPTER TEN

When I learned to Mother God way

As time went by, I began to realize that to truly raise my children in the way they should go, I had to first fix me. I had to learn who Jewel really was not just the mother, the provider, or the survivor but the woman God created. I started to teach myself how to live more modestly, how to respond to insults with grace, how to live in this ungodly world without being of it. I had to discover what made me smile, what brought me peace, and what needed healing inside me..

I began to study the Word of God as if I were in college. deeply, intentionally, daily. I wasn't just reading scriptures anymore I was digesting them. I was learning how to apply them to my life and to the way I mothered. I wanted my home to reflect the presence of God, so I turned it into a sanctuary.

I realized I hadn't always been the mother I should've been. I raised my firstborn, Jaliya, while still trying to live a life I wasn't ready to let go of.

I was young, caught up in the world, trying to balance motherhood while still wanting to be a "girl." I didn't always have patience. I didn't know then what I know now. And when she left the home, it gave me the space

I needed to examine myself, not in shame but in honesty. I couldn't change the past, but I could change how I parented moving forward.

I started with myself. I learned to be more patient, more present. I began playing the Bible aloud while the children slept, filling our home with

God's Word. I prayed over my children daily even Jaliya when she was still with me. I would lay hands on them and cry out to God for guidance and protection. I created a rhythm of worship in our home playing praise music, speaking scriptures, and praying together as a family.

We made it a tradition to say Psalm 91 every single night before bed. We all memorized it by heart:

"Those who live in the shelter of the Most High will find rest in the shadow of the Almighty."

— Psalm 91:1 NLT

It became our family's covering. We slept in peace because we knew God's protection was over us.

I also began spending more intentional time with each child asking them how they were feeling, checking in emotionally and spiritually. I was no longer just "doing my job" as a mother. I was being a mother nurturing, listening, and guiding.

My landscaping and property preservation business gave me the flexibility to be home and pour into my children. That was divine alignment. I realized God had given me this season not just to build a business, but to build legacy starting inside my home.

I taught my kids who God was, how to treat people, and how to recognize their own worth. I explained to them that yes, life would still come with trials, but they had a strong tower to run to. I wanted them to know how to stand strong even when I'm no longer here. Because one day, they will have to face the world without me, and I want them equipped with something no one can take from them faith.

I'm not perfect, but every day I strive to live a life that's pleasing to God.

I decided to follow Him fully, and ever since, my life has only gone up step by step toward the top of Zion. He hasn't dropped me yet.

> *"Train up a child in the way he should go, and when he is old, he will not depart from it."*
>
> **— Proverbs 22:6 NLT**

I realized there were things within myself I needed to confront patterns I never asked for but had carried with me for years. My parents didn't hug me. They didn't ask if I was okay. I don't remember being shown warmth or affection in a way that made me feel emotionally safe. And for a long time, I didn't think I needed it. I thought providing and protecting were enough.

But as I started feeding my spirit with the Word of God, it began to expose what had gone unnoticed. The Word became a mirror, not just for how I was living, but how I was parenting. It didn't shame me. It shaped me. It gently showed me the areas I needed to grow not just for my children's sake, but for mine.

As I looked back, I saw how that emotional absence from my childhood had carried into my motherhood especially with my firstborn. If she got mad at me, I got mad right back. I'd shut down, and she would too. I couldn't understand why she was upset when I made sure she had everything she needed food, clothes, a roof over her head. But now I understand. Children don't just need provision. They need presence. They need softness. They need connection.

That understanding changed me.

Now when my children are upset, I don't react with frustration. I take a breath. I give us both a moment. And then I come back and ask, "What's wrong? Tell me what you're feeling." I ask them to help me see things from their perspective. That one shift alone has opened doors between us that used to be locked shut.

I also had to reflect on how protective I was. I didn't want my children going anywhere. I didn't want anything or anyone to hurt them. I thought keeping them close always was the best way to love them. But I started to see that control isn't the same as care. And while some of my children could understand and adapt to that type of parenting, Jaliya couldn't. She felt suffocated. She needed freedom. And back then, I didn't know how to give it in a way that felt safe to me.

But as my other children got older, I became more open. More understanding. More willing to listen. I let them go places within reason and maturity once I felt they were old enough to defend themselves and make wise choices. It was still hard. But I didn't lead from fear anymore. I led from wisdom.

And then came a moment that showed me just how much I had changed.

One day, I got a call that my youngest son was acting out at school. Badly. The old me might've gone straight to correction or taken it as a reflection of my parenting. But this time, I paused. I remembered everything I had learned. I saw this as my second chance an opportunity to handle this moment with grace and patience, not frustration.

I sat him down, looked him in his eyes, and gently asked, "What's bothering you?" I didn't rush him. I gave him space to process and respond. I could tell it made a difference. Just being heard gave him the comfort to open, even when he didn't fully know how to explain his feelings. But that moment planted a seed that began to grow. Day by day, his behavior improved. He felt seen. Supported. Loved.

That's the fruit of mothering God's way.

It's not about being perfect. It's about being present. It's about being led by the Spirit, not by stress. It's about letting the Word of God parent you, so you can parent your children in love and truth.

I still have moments where I reflect on how I wish I could've parented

Jaliya the way I'm learning to know. That part still stings sometimes. But I don't live in regret. I live in redemption. Because now I know better. And I'm doing better. God didn't just give me more children He gave me another chance to grow.

He's raising me while I raise them.

And I know without a doubt; the legacy I'm building is different now.

My children won't just remember what I gave them they'll remember how I made them feel. They'll remember that their mother walked with God, and because of that, their home was filled with peace, correction, prayer, laughter, and love.

I've learned that true motherhood isn't just a title it's an assignment. And when you accept the assignment God's way, He equips you to carry it out with joy.

As I continued growing in my walk with God, I noticed He was teaching me not just how to parent, but how to lead by example. I had always kept a clean home, kept things in order, and stayed consistent in structure but now, God was showing me how to bring spiritual order into that same space. He reminded me that order without love feels like control, but order with love feels like peace.

So I asked Him daily to teach me how to lead with love.

There were moments when I'd see one of my children get quiet or withdrawn, and instead of brushing it off or assuming they were just in a "mood," I would now sit beside them, ask questions, and just listen. I'd say, "Hey, what's going on?" And wait. I gave them room to express without being judged. That was something I had to learn. I grew up in a home where silence was normal, where no one really checked on your emotions. But I didn't want to repeat that. I wanted to break that cycle.

I didn't want my children growing up holding everything inside just because they didn't feel safe enough to speak. So, I created a safe space a real one. Not just physically, but emotionally. I told them, "You can tell me anything. I might not always agree, but I'm always going to listen with love."

And it started to work.

They began to open up about their fears, about things at school, about their dreams. I began to learn how different each of my children really were. Same mother, same home, same prayers but different hearts, different needs, and different ways they feel loved. That's when I realized mothering God's way isn't about having a one-size-fits-all approach. It's about asking Him, "How do I love each child the way You created them to be loved?"

And day by day, He showed me.

There were times I had to correct them. Times I had to enforce boundaries. But even in correction, I learned to include explanation.

Instead of just saying "Because I said so," I'd say, "Because I love you, and this is why it matters." That shift alone changed everything. They didn't see me as the enemy anymore. They saw me as a guide as someone who wasn't just controlling them but protecting them.

And even though I hadn't always known how to do that when I was younger, I gave myself grace. Because now I did know. And I was doing it.

God reminded me that just like He gives us new mercies every day, I can give myself new mercy too. I didn't have to live in regret. I could live in redemption. I was being redeemed as a woman, and as a mother. And that healing began to show in my household.

As I kept growing in motherhood, I started to understand that everything my children were going through wasn't always just spiritual. Some of it was mental. Some emotional. Some things were rooted in their childhood trauma and some in mine.

I had to stop and say, "Wait a minute this isn't just them acting out. This might be something deeper."

There were times when I looked into their eyes and saw something I couldn't always pray away. I had to slow down and realize they were fighting internal battles I couldn't see. That's when I learned how important it was to approach motherhood not just with prayer, but with compassion, curiosity, and education.

I started to do more research. I asked questions at their schools. I spoke with counselors, I read articles, I paid close attention to their behavior patterns. I started making the connection between mood changes, attention spans, triggers, and even diet.

Because some of what we call "bad behavior" is really unspoken pain.

I realized how mental health plays a big role in how our kids respond to discipline, to change, to stress. And I had to look at how my own parenting had been shaped by things I didn't receive growing up affection, validation, emotional safety. I wasn't taught how to emotionally regulate, so how could I expect my children to know how?

But I was learning now, and I was determined to teach them what I had just learned myself.

Yes, I still prayed. I still anointed their heads with oil. I still covered them in the blood of Jesus. But I also started having deeper conversations with them. I stopped dismissing what they said with "you're just being dramatic" or "get over it." I started saying, "Okay, I hear you. Tell me more."

And that simple shift changed everything.

It gave them the confidence to speak up instead of shutting down. It let them know their emotions were real and that they had a safe space to release them. I didn't want them holding everything inside like I had to do growing up. I wanted them to feel free to feel and then to grow through it with help, not shame.

Some people assume that because I walk with God, everything in my household is always holy and perfect. But the truth is, this is a healing house. A real house. And in this house, we talk about emotions. We talk about forgiveness. We talk about triggers. We talk about mental health. We talk about God. And we talk about growth.

Because all of it matters.

CHAPTER ELEVEN

Bold Enough to Build and Testify

Running my tree and landscaping business became more than just a job it became a life lesson in patience, purpose, and service. It taught me how to deal with all types of people, from all walks of life, and how to present myself with professionalism, even in tough moments. With God's help, and some guidance from my children's father, I learned the ropes of property maintenance, pricing, and customer care. I took those tools and built something stable for me and my children..

But even with stability, I felt something stirring in my spirit. I had time on my hands, and a fire inside of me to share all that God had done. I knew these testimonies every trial, breakthrough, and miracle weren't just for me. They were meant to bless someone else. God doesn't allow pain for no reason. He allows the fire to refine us so we can help light the path for others.

One day I looked at my life and said, "It's time."

Time to open my mouth.

Time to come out of the shadows.

Time to glorify God out loud.

So I turned to the tool in front of me social media.

At first, it started with a modeling video, something my mom once had me do when I was just nine years old. That video went viral. Then I posted a trending dance—I've always loved to dance and that too went viral. Before I knew it, I was getting millions of views. I took those videos, reposted them across all platforms, and suddenly my life changed.

I reached over 30 million views and earned my YouTube play button in under four months. All from just being myself.

But this wasn't about fame. It was about purpose.

I started streaming live not for attention, but for impact. I wanted the world to know that God is still in the miracle-working business. That

He's faithful, trustworthy, and that if you surrender your life to Him, you'll never walk alone. Every live stream became a pulpit. Every comment section, a congregation. Every testimony I shared, a seed planted into someone's life.

God had trusted me with trials. Now he was trusting me with a platform.

And I was ready.

Scriptures that anchored me during this season:

"I will speak of your testimonies before kings and will not be ashamed.

I saw the number 3.3 million in a vision, and I knew it had to mean something. It wasn't just a random number. It was prophetic. It was confirmation that the people God had called me to reach weren't just a handful they were multitudes.

As I began streaming regularly and staying consistent with sharing what God put on my heart, I watched that number begin to manifest in real time. Thousands of people started joining my livestreams. They began commenting things like, "I needed this," or "You just saved my life." People I had never met were tuning in, crying, praying, repenting right there through a phone screen.

God was using me as a vessel to speak light into dark places. My voice, my pain, my testimony it was all a weapon against the enemy. He thought he had me. He thought those hard seasons would break me. He thought those foster care papers, those eviction notices, and those suicidal moments in my daughter would silence me. But all they did was prepare me for this platform.

I didn't just stream for entertainment. I streamed because it became my outlet. My safe place.

I wasn't going out to clubs.

I wasn't hanging out on weekends.

I wasn't around a bunch of friends or even family.

Honestly, I didn't have many people in my corner anymore. I had been betrayed, lied on, gossiped about, and used. My circle was tight because

God had shown me that not everyone who claps for you is clapping from a pure heart. Some want to see you win but not more than them.

So I stayed home. I focused on raising my kids, running my business, and feeding my spirit. And in that quiet space, God grew something loud.

He gave me a voice that could reach homes across the world. People from the UK, Africa, California, New York they were showing up in my comments daily. They would say, "You don't even know me, but what you said tonight saved me from giving up."

That was when I knew this wasn't about me.

This was purpose.

God didn't just give me 3.3 million for nothing. He gave it to me so I could glorify Him. So, I could testify boldly. So I could show people that even someone like me a single mother, misunderstood, once homeless, once broken could rise again through Christ.

And it wasn't long before the real world started to reflect the online world.

I would go to the store or stop at the gas station and someone would walk up with a smile and say, "Aren't you Jewel from online?" They'd ask for pictures, say thank you, share their own stories. And even though it was beautiful, I also had to move wisely.

Because fame even when it's wrapped in purpose can attract both favor and warfare.

There were people who didn't like me, who didn't even know me. Some only knew the version of the story they heard from others, not the truth I had lived. Some judged me for placing my daughter in foster care, not knowing the whole situation. But I had to learn how to keep going. I had to remember what I told God from the beginning: "Use me. I'll speak. I'll go. I'll testify."

So I kept going.

I knew the platform wasn't mine it was borrowed. It was a stage for His glory.

God had assigned me to this generation, and social media was just the tool. He made me bold. He made me relatable. He gave me favor with people who needed to know they weren't alone. Every story I told, every tear I shared, every word of encouragement it was for His kingdom.

This wasn't about going viral. This was about going deeper. Deeper into purpose. Deeper into healing. Deeper into assignment.

Because when God says it's time, you don't need a degree. You don't need a microphone. You don't need a platform built by man.

You just need obedience.

And I had that.

So I streamed through my healing.

I streamed through hard days.

I streamed even when I didn't feel like talking.

Because I wasn't showing up as a character I was showing up as a vessel.

And lives were being changed.

As time went on, I started to notice something else God was not only using streaming to bless others, but He was also using it to bless me too.

My livestreams began bringing in income. What started as a place of healing became a source of provision. I wasn't asking for money. I was just showing up faithfully, and somehow, God touched hearts. People started sowing seeds, giving love offerings, supporting my voice because they believed in the God behind it.

And I didn't take that lightly.

Every dollar that came in through streaming, I handled with intention. I didn't go buy luxury for show I reinvested it into my business. I took that money and bought equipment for my landscaping company. I poured it into branding, materials, uniforms, gas, tools whatever was needed to keep things going. I understood that God gives seed to the Sower, not the selfish.

Streaming gave me flexibility too. I could still be at home with my kids, still take on clients during the week, and still pour into others online at night. I wasn't tied to anyone else's schedule. God gave me freedom, and I used it to build something that could last.

People would say, "How are you doing all this on your own?"

And I'd respond, "It's not just me. It's God, strategy, and obedience."

I learned how to take one open door and walk through it with faith.

That's all it took.

Streaming wasn't just a source of ministry it became a stream of income, a stream of purpose, and a stream of divine favor.

And the more I testified, the more God trusted me with. I could feel it in my spirit this was only the beginning. I was becoming bold, not just online, but in person. I started walking in rooms with confidence. I started speaking life over others the way I wished someone had done for me when I was down and confused.

I wasn't waiting to be asked I was stepping forward.

Because I realized something:

When you're bold enough to build and bold enough to testify God will make sure the right ears hear your voice, and the right hands support your mission.

CHAPTER TWELVE

When God started to reveal my purpose

When I wasn't livestreaming or running my business, I was spending intentional time every single day building my relationship with God. I fell in love with virtual church, prophetic prayer lines, and deep Bible study. I began treating the Word of God like it was a college exam I had to pass studying each scripture, chapter, and book as if my life depended on it..

I joined a daily prayer line, listening to powerful teachings and prophecies. And what blew me away was how many of those prophecies confirmed things I had only whispered to God in prayer things no one else knew about. That's when I knew this wasn't just community, it was divine connection. God was responding.

I remember one moment so clearly my baby hadn't had a bowel movement in several days. As a mother, I was stressed, but instead of panicking, I paused and prayed. I laid my hand on her and spoke healing.

I said, "God, please make my daughter whole. Let her bowels flow as they should. Heal her body." And almost instantly, she went. That moment reminded me of the power of prayer that God really does hear even the smallest of requests.

One day I felt myself growing weary of routine. The landscaping business was steady. Social media was going well. But deep in my spirit, I said to God, "There has to be more You want me to do while I'm here in the land of the living." I cried out to Him and said, "Lord, show me what else You've placed inside me. Reveal Your purpose."

Not long after, a prophet on the prayer line asked if he could speak a word into my life. I was hesitant at first, but I've learned to listen when someone truly carries the voice of God. He began to prophesy that God was going to use me in the marketplace that I would create a handmade product with my own hands. He said it would impact lives and be tied to my calling. Then he revealed other details private things I had spoken only to God about. I was stunned. The Holy Spirit was clearly moving.

At the time, I didn't fully understand what that meant. But weeks later, while I was driving, I had what I believe was my first open vision. Out of nowhere, I saw the words "Hair Growth Oil" appear vividly in front of me. I almost swerved! It startled me but it also gave me peace. God was speaking again, and I knew it.

I didn't have the full plan. I didn't know the name, the ingredients, the label nothing. All I knew was God was guiding me to make this oil, and because of my past experiences, I had learned to follow when He speaks.

I had learned to say "Yes" even when I couldn't see the outcome. I had learned that obedience birth's purpose.

Looking back, I know now God had always been trying to partner with me. He was already living within me, but I had been living by my own will, not His. I used to choose the wrong jobs, wrong men, wrong habits, and still tried to carry the title of "strong." But when I finally allowed the Holy Spirit to lead, my eyes opened. I realized that I didn't have to carry the burden alone. And I didn't have to keep guessing my way through life.

God started to show me who I really was not broken, not lost, not overlooked, but chosen. He started to pull the veil back and reveal that I was created to build, serve, lead, and testify. Not just for me but to glorify Him and help others break free.

One thing about God when He begins to reveal your purpose, He does it in ways that leave no room for doubt.

As I stayed in His Word, He started speaking to me in very specific ways. I wasn't googling anything. I wasn't searching YouTube for formulas. I was simply doing what I always did reading my Bible and certain herbs and plants began to pop off the pages. Scriptures that I had read many times before started to come alive in a new way. I would see a word or a plant in the Word of God, and my spirit would pause. I'd underline it, write it down, and ask, "Lord, are You showing me something?"

Then I'd close my Bible and go about my day. But moments later, I'd open my phone and without searching another ingredient would appear in front of me. It could be a sponsored ad, a reel, a caption, or a post. Something completely random but directly tied to what I had just seen in scripture. That's how I knew it was God. He was connecting the dots in a way no one else could. It wasn't a coincidence. It was confirmation.

I didn't question it. I just kept collecting the pieces as He gave them.

I would write the names down in my notebook, and before I knew it, I had a list forming. And I knew I was being given divine instruction. God wasn't just calling me to make a product. He was giving me the formula through spiritual revelation.

And because He gave it to me that way, I knew I had to treat it with reverence. This wasn't just something to throw in a bottle and rush to market. This was something that needed to be made with prayer, obedience, and patience.

So I moved slowly and carefully, checking with God at every step. He began showing me how to package the product. What colors to use.

What words to place on the label. I didn't rush to launch. I waited until I had peace. I waited until I had clear instruction. Because I didn't want this oil to just be another item on a shelf, I wanted it to be a seed of healing, a point of faith, a physical reminder that God is still speaking, still restoring, and still partnering with His daughters to bring Heaven to earth.

I kept praying as I prepared. I laid hands on the bottles. I worshipped while pouring. I let my kids help label, reminding them that this was a family legacy, not just mommy's product. I wanted them to see that purpose can be birthed right in your living room when God is in the center of it.

That's when I began to understand something deeper:

Purpose isn't always loud. It doesn't always come with applause. Sometimes it starts in private between you, God, and your quiet yes. But that yes? It will open doors you never imagined.

I was no longer chasing blessings. I was walking in obedience and blessings were chasing me.

God was starting to reveal not just what I could do with my hands, but what He had planted in my heart long ago. And it wasn't just about oil. It was about faith, healing, surrender, and trust.

He was showing me that my life had never been random. That every trial, every lesson, every lonely moment was leading to this revelation that I was called to create, to build, to serve, and to glorify Him through every assignment.

And I knew, without a doubt, that I had only scratched the surface.

Sooner than I realized, everything God had shown me began to come together. The ingredients He revealed, the packaging He inspired, the name He whispered in my spirit it all aligned. I had a ready-made product in my hands, and it wasn't just any product. It was purpose in a bottle.

Just Unique Love Hair Growth Oil was born not out of strategy, but out of surrender. It came from long nights of prayer, early mornings in the Word, and faith steps I took even when I couldn't see the full picture.

And now, what started as a vision was ready to bless others. What God gave to me in private was about to impact the public. This was just the beginning of what obedience could birth.

CHAPTER THIRTEEN

My Yes Led to Overflow

S o, as the weeks went by, God began to reveal specific ingredients and herbs things I knew He wanted me to use in the hair growth oil. I wrote them down every time He dropped one in my spirit. One time, I was sitting on my couch, and suddenly an article popped up on my phone about hair and natural remedies. I hadn't searched for anything like that it just appeared. It felt like God was confirming, "Yes, daughter, this is the way. Walk in it." It was as if He was guiding my every step through signs, wonders, and quiet revelations.

I began buying and gathering all the ingredients I'd need to bring the vision to life. I had never made a product before never built a website, never shipped an order. But I had something even greater: faith. I walked by faith the entire time. I mixed the ingredients, prayed over them, and created the oil. I tried it on my hair, then on my children. It worked! It healed my daughter's dry scalp and grew her hair. It made my hair stronger and more moisturized. I saw growth. I saw healing.

Then I gifted bottles to my parents, my children's grandmother and it worked for them, too. I waited several months, just observing, trusting.

Once I knew this oil wasn't just a coincidence but a God-given creation, I released it to the marketplace. The same day I launched, I sold out. Orders poured in. Within my first year, I had made my first six figures all from a vision, obedience, and trust.

When I say, "our business," I mean me and God. Because I would've never created a hair care brand on my own. I wasn't chasing trends. I was chasing obedience. I used the oil to bless others, gifting it through giveaways and even using it in prayer. People would message me saying the oil healed skin conditions, helped with joint pain, even emotional relief. I realized: this is more than a hair product this is a miracle in a bottle.

One night, God gave me a dream about business cards. But they weren't just cards they had scriptures on them. He showed me exactly how they should look. So, I created them. Now, every customer receives one with Psalms 91 and 27, the very scriptures my kids and I pray nightly. It became part of the testimony. God was using everything my hands, my pain, my faith, and even packaging for His glory. I was just the vessel.

And while everything looked peaceful on the outside, I still had trials. Delays came. Attacks came. But I had seen God move before. And if He did it before, He'd do it again. I was grateful to be chosen.

My mindset wasn't to stay stuck. I wasn't created to stay dormant, waiting for trouble to push me into motion. I was born to elevate to keep growing, keep building, keep believing. Whether it was in my health, my parenting, my finances, or my relationship with God, I knew I was meant to rise like an eagle.

Chickens might flap around, barely getting off the ground but eagles soar above the storms. That's the mindset I chose. I wasn't settling. I wasn't shrinking. I was climbing higher in the Word, higher in wisdom, and higher in purpose.

To do that, I had to believe in myself. I had to gain confidence in who God said I was. And I had to say "Yes" even when I was afraid. That "yes" was the door to overflow.

I kept hearing God say, "Stay faithful in the little, and I will make you ruler over much." So, I stayed faithful. Even when only one order came in that day, I packed it with care. I anointed every bottle, prayed over it, and shipped it with expectation. I knew I wasn't just mailing out oil i was sending out obedience. I was sending out healing. I was sending out purpose. And because of that, I never looked at small numbers as failure i saw them as foundation.

I remember one night crying in prayer, asking God when things would really shift. And He said so clearly to my spirit, "I'm not just growing your brand, I'm growing you." That changed everything for me. I stopped chasing success and started embracing process. I stopped comparing my timeline to others and started trusting the pace God had me on. It was personal. He wasn't just trying to make me a business owner he was making me a Kingdom builder.

Month after month, I began to see the increase. Not just in sales, but in clarity, confidence, and capacity. I was learning how to manage inventory, how to market effectively, how to connect with customers in a genuine way. I created content with intention not just to sell, but to share my story and encourage someone else to keep going.

And sure enough, overflow came.

I watched God turn a few orders into hundreds. I saw my notifications light up with people saying, "Your oil is growing my edges back," or "This product is restoring my confidence." The same oil that started as a vision in my spirit was now blessing others in real life. That's how I knew it wasn't just a business it was ministry. It was a seed planted in faith that was now bearing fruit.

Financial doors began opening. I no longer feared lack. I no longer questioned how I would provide. I knew now that I was called to be the head and not the tail, a lender and not a borrower. And the beautiful thing is I didn't get here by hustling for man's approval. I got here by saying "yes" to God. By showing up daily with an open heart and surrendered hands.

Now I run my business with purpose, knowing that every order has a story, every bottle has a breakthrough tied to it. And I'm not done yet this is just the beginning. I believe that if I stay in alignment with God, the overflow will continue. Not just in sales, but in impact. Because what

God starts, He sustains. And when you say yes to Him, He'll take your obedience and multiply it beyond what you could ever imagine.

CHAPTER FOURTEEN

I finally got my dream truck then a squirrel chewed the wires

There's something about walking in alignment with God that brings a peace and confidence you can't explain. My business was thriving. Our oil orders were flowing in. I was consistent in prayer, consistent in tithing, and felt like I was finally experiencing the reward of obedience. For once, I wasn't just surviving I was living.

We were in our beautiful new home, a blessing I didn't take lightly. But every time I pulled into my driveway in that old 2013 Honda Odyssey leaking oil on my freshly poured concrete, I felt a tug. That van had carried us through a lot, but it didn't match this new season. I didn't need anything flashy. I just needed something reliable, something safe for my kids and I. But deep down I also desired something I had never dared to ask for before: my dream truck.

I had my eye on it for over a year and a half. I would see it on the road and whisper, "One day." I'm not the type to treat myself I'll spend everything on my kids, buy gifts for others, pour into people. But this time, I prayed about it. I didn't want to move ahead of God, but I also knew I had been faithful. I wasn't chasing material things. I was just ready for something dependable that also aligned with where He was taking me.

So, one day, without overthinking, I got up and went to the dealership. I told myself, "I'm going to test drive it. Just see." But God had already made the way. I walked out with the keys to my dream SUV everything I wanted and more. My heart was full. I felt like I was finally receiving the overflow.

But a few months later, everything changed.

One day, I noticed the smart features weren't working the sensors, the backup camera, all the things that made the truck "luxury." I took it in, thinking maybe it was a system reset or something minor. What they found? A squirrel had gotten into the hood and chewed through the smart wiring.

I couldn't believe it. A squirrel?

They kept the truck at the dealership to repair it. What should've been a simple fix turned into a waiting game that lasted four months. Four months without my dream vehicle. Four months of being reminded that no matter how high you climb, the enemy will still try to pull you down. I remember sitting in my driveway some nights asking God, "Why now? Why this?" I wasn't mad. I was just confused. I thought we were past these battles.

But faith doesn't come without warfare. And elevation doesn't exempt you from trials. If anything, it increases them.

Still, I stayed faithful. Still, I kept praying. Still, I kept showing up to the post office, dropping off oil packages, smiling at customers, trusting that God had a reason for this. And it was in one of those simple moments no cameras, no spotlight just me doing what God told me to do, that He sent confirmation.

I was walking out of the post office when I crossed paths with a man walking on foot. I didn't know him, but something about him felt spiritual. He stopped and looked at me. And I'll never forget his words.

He said, "That truck is going to be paid off. And you're going to get a new one."

I didn't ask him for a word. I didn't tell him what was happening. He had no way of knowing. But the moment he said it; I felt the Spirit of God all over me. It was a whisper from Heaven: "I see you. I got this."

Weeks later, I got a call. Not from the dealership but from the actual manufacturer of my vehicle. They apologized for the delay, acknowledged they couldn't fix the problem, and then they said something I'll never forget:

"We're going to pay off your current vehicle in full. We're cutting you a check. And we're replacing it with a brand-new one."

I sat there stunned. God did it again.

What started as a frustrating, seemingly random trial ended as a miracle. God didn't just restore what was broken He upgraded it. He didn't just fix the situation He proved that even a squirrel can't block what He has for His children.

This chapter of my life reminded me: Just because you're walking in purpose doesn't mean trials won't show up. But when they do, God shows up greater. What was meant to discourage me only made me trust Him more.

I started reflecting on how far I had come. This wasn't my first storm. I had already lived through worse from not knowing where we would sleep, to standing inside a home that I owned. I had trusted God through homelessness, heartbreak, loss, and brokenness. And He never failed me.

So even in this situation even when my brand-new truck was in a shop for months and I was back to driving borrowed vehicles or finding rides I chose to believe that God was still in control. I didn't feel embarrassed. I didn't care what anyone might've assumed. I knew the truth: God gave me that vehicle, and if He allowed this interruption, there had to be a reason.

Sometimes we equate new trials with failure. But I had learned by now that obedience doesn't mean a trial won't show up it means God will get the glory out of it when it does.

It was frustrating, yes. Four months without the vehicle I had waited so long for. Four months of calling and checking and hoping for updates. But it wasn't about the SUV anymore it became about how I would respond. Would I panic? Would I doubt? Or would I stand on everything I knew to be true about the God I serve?

I kept choosing faith. I kept mailing packages. I kept speaking life into others while quietly trusting God for my own miracle.

That moment with the prophet at the post office stayed in my spirit. I hadn't shared my situation. I didn't ask for a word. But God saw me and sent encouragement in a place I least expected a reminder that He was still working behind the scenes.

I hung up the phone and just sat there in silence. Not because I didn't have anything to say, but because I knew what had just happened wasn't normal it was supernatural. I could feel the presence of God wrap around me like a blanket. The kind of peace you can't explain. The kind of confirmation that reminds you: God saw it all. And He handled it.

In that moment, I wasn't thinking about the inconvenience I had just gone through. I wasn't replaying the stress of not having my vehicle or the weeks of calls and updates. I was standing in awe of a God who didn't just give me back what I lost He gave me more than I had before.

He cleared the balance. No car note. No debt. He gave me a brand-new replacement vehicle same model, better condition, better outcome. And He did it in a way that only He could take credit for.

It's not just that He provided. It's how He did it through a word from a prophet at the post office, through a manufacturer that rarely does things like this, through a situation I never could've orchestrated on my own.

I felt God reminding me: "This is why I told you to wait on Me. This is why I said don't give up. This is what happens when you trust Me even in the trials."

And I don't want to lie I had a moment where I smiled to myself and said, "Look at God." Not out of pride, but from a place of knowing what it cost me to get here. I thought back to the seasons when I didn't even have a car. The bus routes. The borrowed rides. The times I walked with groceries and kids. And now... He had brought me full circle.

I think about how sometimes we're tempted to question God when something breaks. But what if the breakdown is the very thing that triggers the blessing?

What if that squirrel didn't destroy my truck what if God allowed it so He could upgrade what I thought I had to settle for?

Because yes, I loved that truck. It was my dream. But maybe even that wasn't the final version God wanted for me. Maybe He had a better one in store the whole time — and He used something as small and unexpected as a squirrel to make room for it.

That'll humble you.

It reminded me that God really does work in the details. The things we overlook, the things we think are frustrating or random He's using them. Nothing is wasted. Not the waiting. Not the breakdown. Not the months of silence. Not even the pest chewing through wires. He knows how to use everything.

This wasn't just a testimony about a car. It was a testimony about faith under fire. A reminder that even when you're living right, even when you're walking in purpose, you'll still face tests. But those tests come to prove that your foundation is solid.

God knew I wouldn't break during those four months. He knew I would keep going, keep praying, keep working, keep encouraging others even when I was dealing with discouragement myself. And because of that, He didn't just restore me He elevated me.

Now when I look at my new truck, I smile. Not because it's luxury, but because it's evidence. Evidence that God takes care of His children. Evidence that obedience is never in vain. Evidence that when you trust Him with the details, He'll surprise you in ways that leave you speechless.

So many people think once you step into your purpose, the hard seasons just disappear. But the truth is, purpose attracts pressure. Elevation invites attack. The more aligned you are with God's will, the more the enemy tries to shake your faith.

But what the enemy didn't realize was I was unshakable.

Not because of my own strength, but because of the God who holds me steady. He allowed the storm to come, but He never let it overtake me. He used the inconvenience to reveal His intention. And He proved, once again, that obedience opens doors no man can shut.

Now that I look back, I don't believe that moment was just about a car. It was about positioning. I felt deep in my spirit that God was setting me up for His next huge move. This blessing wasn't just to make me smile it was to prepare me for what was coming.

So I took that check they gave me the one they issued to pay off the old truck and I didn't touch it. I placed it straight into my savings. Not out of fear, but out of faith. Because I know how God works. He is strategic, omniscient, and always intentional. Nothing He allows is wasted. Every interruption, every inconvenience, every closed door it's all part of a greater setup.

I've learned to stop asking "why" and start expecting what's next. Because when God allows something to fall apart, it's usually because something greater is about to come together.

Even if it looks like a setback, even if it feels unfair keep walking. Keep trusting. Because the very thing sent to break you may just be the thing God uses to bless you.

I don't know who this chapter is for but if you're going through something that doesn't make sense right now, I want you to hold on to this promise:

"The Lord will fight for you; you need only to be still."

— Exodus 14:14 (NLT)

Still your fears. Still your assumptions. Still your need to control the outcome. God is already working it out in ways you can't even see. The weapon may form but it will not prosper.

Because you were never meant to just go through it.

You were chosen to overcome it.

CHAPTER FIFTEEN

Crowned for the Calling

There comes a moment in your journey when you realize everything you went through was preparing you to carry something greater something divine. I didn't just survive the trials. I was transformed by them. I didn't just get through I grew through every loss, every closed door, every prayer I had to whisper through tears. What once looked like defeat was really God refining me. And now, I understand it was never just about the blessings I would receive. It was about becoming the woman who could carry the calling.

From being homeless with three children and no help, to owning my own home, launching a six-figure business, and stepping boldly into ministry I know without a doubt, I have been crowned for the calling. Not because I'm perfect. Not because I had it all together. But because I said "yes" to God.

I look back at the moments I didn't think I'd make it, and I now see how

God was always nearby. Even when I felt unseen and unheard by the world, Heaven was still speaking. God was writing my story with every painful pause and every silent stretch.

To the reader who made it to this page, I want you to know something:

You are needed. You are wanted. You are loved.

There is purpose on your life. Even if no one else ever told you that before hearing it now, from someone who has been through the fire and came out refined: You are not here by accident.

The storms you're facing?

They are only temporary.

If you give all your pain, ideas, problems, cares, burdens, and thoughts to the Lord God, He will surely acknowledge them. He will start to guide you into the very purpose you were created for. Not one ounce of your suffering will be wasted.

We're not perfect. We may fall short of the glory of God sometimes. But every day, you have a new chance to pick up your cross, die to the flesh, and live a life filled with purpose. Start by filling your spirit read the Word, play positive music, and surround yourself with people who uplift your soul.

Ask God to give you the gift of discernment so you'll recognize His voice, know who is truly for you, and be able to see clearly when deception tries to come in. If you find yourself in a dark place again, don't wait. Immediately call on the name of God.

Say Psalms 91 out loud and declare His promises over your life. For at the name of Jesus, every enemy must flee.

"No weapon formed against you shall prosper."

— Isaiah 54:17 (NLT)

Let this be your reminder: the same God who crowned me with purpose, after all I went through, can do the same for you.

You're not too far gone.

You're not too broken.

You're not too late.

You're right on time.

He's just waiting on your "yes."

Declaration + Prayer for the Reader

Speak this over yourself daily whether you're at the mountaintop or in the valley:

"I am chosen. I am healed. I am whole. I am loved. I am covered by the blood of Jesus. I will live and not die. I will declare the works of the Lord. I am the head and not the tail. I am above only and not beneath. I am anointed for this. I am crowned for the calling."

Now let's pray:

Father God,

Thank You for the one reading this. I ask that You remind them daily that they were born with purpose. Let them know they are never alone, even in their darkest seasons. Strengthen them where they are weak and pour fresh oil on the dry places of their soul. I pray that their yes unlocks everything You've had prepared for them since before they were in their mother's womb.

Surround them with Your favor like a shield. Let no weapon formed against them prosper.

Help them to hear You clearly, walk boldly, and trust fully.

Thank You for carrying them through every storm, and thank You in advance for their testimony that will come out of this season.

In Jesus' name, Amen.

7-DAY DEVOTIONAL: CHOSEN ON PURPOSE

Day 1 – You Were Never Forgotten

Scripture: Exodus 14:14 (NLT)

Encouragement: Even in your most silent seasons, God never left you. What felt like isolation was preparation.

Reflection: Where in your life do you need to let go and let God take over?

Prayer: Lord, remind me that Your presence never left me. Help me to trust You even when I feel alone. Amen.

Day 2 – Trusting His Timing

Scripture: Ecclesiastes 3:11 (NLT)

Encouragement: God's delays are not His denials. He's developing strength, faith, and character within you.

Reflection: Can you recall a time when God's timing was better than your own?

Prayer: Father, teach me to wait with expectation, knowing You make all things beautiful in Your time. Amen.

Day 3 – Beauty from Ashes

Scripture: Isaiah 61:3 (NLT)

Encouragement: Your pain is never wasted. God is in the business of restoration.

Reflection: What broken place in your life is God healing or has already healed?

Prayer: God, thank You for turning my ashes into beauty. Amen.

Day 4 – Strength in Surrender

Scripture: 2 Corinthians 12:10 (NLT)

Encouragement: Letting go doesn't make you weak — it opens the door for God's strength to show up.

Reflection: What have you been holding on to that God is asking you to surrender?

Prayer: Lord, I give You the things I can't carry anymore. Be strong in me. Amen.

Day 5 – Walking in Purpose

Scripture: Romans 8:28 (NLT)

Encouragement: Nothing in your life is wasted — not one tear, not one detour.

Reflection: What has God used from your past to lead you into purpose?

Prayer: God, show me how every part of my journey was pointing me back to You. Amen.

Day 6 – Grace for the Journey

Scripture: 2 Corinthians 12:9 (NLT)

Encouragement: You don't have to be perfect to be used by God. His grace fills the gap.

Reflection: Where do you need to stop striving and receive God's grace?

Prayer: Jesus, I rest in Your grace. Amen.

Day 7 – Victory Belongs to You

Scripture: Psalm 28:8 (NLT)

Encouragement: There is anointing in your scars and victory in your surrender.

Reflection: How has God already shown you you're victorious?

Prayer: Thank You, God, for calling me victorious. Help me to walk like I already won. Amen.

YOUR TESTIMONIES & TRIUMPHS

U se this space to write down every trial, test, and storm that God brought you through. Leave room to record the dates when your prayers were answered or your dreams come true. Let this page remind you that God is still writing your story, and the best is yet to come.

ABOUT THE AUTHOR

Jewel Nalls

J ewel Nalls is a WOG mother of five, entrepreneur, and the founder of Just Unique Love LLC. After overcoming homelessness, heartbreak, and the battles of single motherhood, Jewel turned her trials into triumphs. Now a homeowner, businesswoman, and author, she shares her testimony to help others rise in faith, restore their identity, and walk boldly into purpose.